DEBT COLLECTION PRACTICE in CALIFORNIA

VOLUMES 1 & 2

Update
December 1997

AUTHOR and EDITOR
Jane H. Fabian
CEB Attorney

CEB

CONTINUING EDUCATION OF THE BAR ▪ BERKELEY, CALIFORNIA

Book Authors
Harold B. Auerbach
Lawrence M. Freiser, CEB Attorney
Darrel C. Horsted
Deane B. Houston
Robert B. Kaplan
Judith A. Levitt
Iain A. Macdonald
David Naftalin
Raymond M. Taketa
Leslie J. Tchaikovsky

Book Editors
Brad Bunnin, CEB Attorney
Victor L. Chuan
Charles D. Daly
Lawrence M. Freiser, CEB Attorney
Edward D. Giacomini, CEB Attorney
Kathleen H. Hartley
Paul I. Peyrat, CEB Attorney
Craig H. Scott, CEB Attorney

Library of Congress Catalog Card No. 87–70327

Printed in the United States of America
ISBN 0–7626–0165–5

BU-30811

CEB

CONTINUING EDUCATION OF THE BAR ▪ CALIFORNIA

By agreement between the Board of Governors of the State Bar of California and The Regents of the University of California, Continuing Education of the Bar – California offers an educational program for the benefit of practicing lawyers. The program is administered by a Governing Committee through the University of California in cooperation with local bar associations and the Joint Advisory Committee made up of the State Bar Committee on Continuing Education of the Bar and the Deans of accredited law schools.

Practice books are published as part of the educational program. Authors are given full opportunity to express their individual legal interpretations and opinions, and these obviously are not intended to reflect any position of the State Bar of California or of the University of California. Chapters written by employees of state or federal agencies are not to be considered statements of governmental policies.

Continuing Education of the Bar – California publications and oral programs are intended to provide current and accurate information about the subject matter covered and are designed to help attorneys maintain their professional competence. Publications are distributed and oral programs presented with the understanding that CEB does not render any legal, accounting, or other professional service. Attorneys using CEB publications or orally conveyed information in dealing with a specific client's or their own legal matters should also research original sources of authority.

Preface

This update, like most CEB publications, was produced by and for members of the California Bar. Members of the Bar wrote and edited it, and the problems were discussed with California lawyers.

We consider this update part of a dialogue with our readers. Another update next year, cumulative of this one, will give us an opportunity to make corrections and additions you suggest. If you know something we did not include, or if we erred, share your knowledge with other California lawyers. Send your comments to:

Update Editor
Continuing Education of the Bar—California
2300 Shattuck Avenue
Berkeley, California 94704

CEB Attorney Jane H. Fabian wrote this year's update.

Legal research assistance was provided by Alan Flatt and Kate Shep-pard. Paul Green handled copyediting and production. The index was updated by the indexing staff. Composition was performed by CEB's Electronic Publishing staff.

This update contains, in addition to its own index and table of forms, corrected versions of the Book index and table of forms.

Craig A. Conly
Interim Director

Pamela J. Jester
Interim Co-Director

Contents

Selected Developments

DEBT COLLECTION PRACTICE IN CALIFORNIA
December 1997 Update

Since Last Update: Effective January 1, 1997, CC §1770(b) makes it an unfair or deceptive act or practice for a mortgage broker or lender to use a home improvement contractor to negotiate the terms of any loan used to finance a home improvement contract that is secured by the borrower's residence. See Update §2.47.

Also effective January 1, 1997, Bus & P C §7507.9(i) allows a repossession agency to request written authorization from the debtor or the legal owner to release personal property not covered by a security interest to someone other than the debtor. See Update §2.65.

An appellate court has held that, when a motion to transfer an action to superior court from municipal court is denied, the aggrieved party may obtain appellate review on appeal from the final judgment entered by the municipal court. See Update §3.4.

Constables are no longer defined as levying officers. Former Govt C §§27820–27829 have been repealed. See Update §3.37.

Code of Civil Procedure §564(b)(11) now authorizes appointment of a receiver in an action brought by an assignee with an assignment of leases under CC §2938(g). See Update §5.41.

Effective January 1, 1997, when a keeper is placed in a business for the purpose of taking into custody tangible personal property consisting solely of money or equivalent proceeds of sales, the levying officer is now authorized to take the property into exclusive custody at the end of each daily keeper period. CCP §700.070(c). This is an exception to the rule in CCP §700.070(b)(1)–(3) regarding when the levying officer is to take tangible personal property into custody. See Update §7.23.

In a potentially far-reaching decision, the Ninth Circuit has held that service of the order to appear for an examination creates a lien and that no further steps to perfect the lien are required. See *In re Hilde* (Zimmerman v Southern Cal. Bank) (9th Cir 1997) 120 F3d 950, in Update §§8.7, 8.19.

In *In re Rawlinson* (Rawlinson v Kendall) (Bankr 9th Cir 1997) 209 BR 501, the Ninth Circuit Bankruptcy Appellate Panel held that an IRA could be claimed as exempt under CCP §703.140(b)(10)(E) (as a "similar plan or contract"). See Update §9.27A.

Effective December 1, 1997, certain Federal Rules of Civil Procedure regarding jury trials are applicable in bankruptcy courts. See Update §10.4.

The Ninth Circuit has held that, for purposes of determining whether a transfer is avoidable as a preference, the date of transfer of a cashier's check is the date of delivery. *In re Lee* (Hall-Mark Elecs. Corp. v Sims) (9th Cir 1997) 108 F3d 239. See Update §10.51.

Since Publication of Book: Civil Code §1526 has been added to clarify the law regarding accord and satisfaction of disputed debts. See Update §1.4.

There have been a number of cases interpreting the Song-Beverly Consumer Warranty Act. See Update §§2.104–2.105.

Effective July 1, 1995, the Personal Property Brokers Law (Fin C §§22000–22654), the Consumer Finance Lenders Law (Fin C §§24000–24634), and the Commercial Finance Lenders Law (Fin C §§26000–26653) were consolidated and renamed the California Finance Lenders Law in Fin C §§22000–22780. See Update §§2.59, 2.63, 2.71–2.75, 2.111.

The court of appeal has discussed a creditor's duties under Com C §9504. See Update §3.31.

The term "person" in CCP §481.170 now includes a limited liability company. See Update §4.14.

There are new time limits on the service of papers regarding applications for attachment. See Update §§4.24, 4.26.

Under CCP §485.010, a debtor's "insolvency" now can be used to support a finding of great or irreparable injury to the creditor for the purpose of attaching the debtor's property. See Update §4.67.

There are new procedures for obtaining default judgments (Update §6.6) and new rules to make attorneys more accountable for their own conduct when that conduct is the basis for a motion for relief from default. See Update §6.12.

Code of Civil Procedure §437c(f) was amended to provide that summary adjudication may be granted only if it completely disposes of a cause of action. See Update §6.25.

The court of appeal has discussed the equitable power of a court to amend a judgment to add a judgment debtor. See Update §6.30.

Judgments for child or spousal support are now exempt from any requirement that judgments be renewed. See Update §§6.68, 12.2.

There are new rules governing earnings withholding orders. See Update §§7.17, 7.73, 7.75, 7.81–7.83.

The court of appeal has discussed the debtor's right to claim exemptions following issuance of a turnover order. See Update §8.19. Another court of appeal has discussed when a third party's denial of a debt owed to a judgment debtor is made in bad faith. See Update §8.27.

The judgment creditor may now demand production of documents from the judgment debtor to aid enforcement of the judgment. See Update §8.34A. There are also new rules on written interrogatories submitted to the judgment creditor. See Update §8.34.

The Bankruptcy Reform Act of 1994 was signed into law in October 1994. The changes made by that Act are dealt with throughout Update chap 10, along with other recent developments in the bankruptcy area.

The Ninth Circuit issued its opinion in *In re Pladson* (Kendall v Pladson) (9th Cir 1994) 35 F3d 462, deciding once and for all that the homestead exemption is available to a debtor in a bankruptcy case. See Update §§9.27, 10.20.

The Ninth Circuit has held that a default judgment entered in Florida could be given collateral estoppel effect in a nondischargeability action filed in bankruptcy court in California. See Update §10.32.

The court of appeal has discussed the burden of proof in a third party claim procedure when a creditor opposes the third party's claim on the grounds that the property has been fraudulently transferred to the third party. The court also has discussed the limitations on discovery and the right to a jury trial in a third party claim procedure. See Update §11.36.

Cutoff Dates

We completed legal editing on this update at the end of August 1997. We reviewed case citations through these cutoffs:

- Shepard's California Citations at 15 C4th 231, 53 CA4th 1126, 136 L Ed 2d 860, 108 F3d 354, 952 F Supp 830.
- Shepard's United States Citations at 136 L Ed 2d 860, 108 F3d 354, 952 F Supp 830.
- Shepard's Federal Citations at 136 L Ed 2d 860, 108 F3d 354, 952 F Supp 830.

We reviewed California and federal statute citations for amendments and repeals through these cutoffs:

- Stats 1997, ch 9.
- 111 Stat 15.

We try to add significant statutory and judicial developments, subsequent histories of cases, and other matters such as new forms and regulations after legal editing is done, but you should not assume that all developments after the listed cutoff dates have been included.

1

Representing the Creditor

[§1.1] SCOPE OF BOOK

Collection cases filed in superior court will be subject to the Trial Court Delay Reduction Act (Govt C §§68600–68620). After July 1, 1992, the Act was in effect in all superior courts in California. Govt C §68605.5. After July 1, 1992, municipal and justice courts were also required to establish delay reduction programs consistent with the Trial Court Delay

Reduction Act. Govt C §68620. Attorneys should check local rules implementing the Act and be alert for changes. For a thorough discussion of the Act and local rules, see Litigation in the Fast Lane: Rules, Analysis, and Practice Guide for Local Programs Mandated Under the Trial Court Delay Reduction Act (Cal CEB 1988).

Although the Book briefly touches on the enforcement of certain family court judgments and orders, this matter is generally beyond the Book's scope. For a comprehensive discussion of this subject, see Practice Under the California Family Code, chap 17 (Cal CEB annual).

1, 2 California Civil Procedure Before Trial (2d ed Cal CEB 1977, 1978) have been replaced by 1, 2, 3 California Civil Procedure Before Trial (3d ed Cal CEB 1990).

1, 2 California Civil Procedure During Trial (Cal CEB 1982, 1984) have been replaced by 1, 2, 3 California Trial Practice: Civil Procedure During Trial (3d ed Cal CEB 1995).

OFFICE MANAGEMENT FOR EFFECTIVE DEBT COLLECTION

Office Procedures

Litigation Forms

[§1.11] Using Predrafted, Judicial Council, and Local Forms

1 California Civil Procedure Before Trial, chap 22 (Cal CEB 1977) has been replaced by 1 California Civil Procedure Before Trial, chap 1 (3d ed Cal CEB 1990).

2 California Civil Procedure Before Trial, chap 23 (Cal CEB 1978) has been replaced by 1 California Civil Procedure Before Trial, chaps 9–11 (3d ed Cal CEB 1990).

PRACTICE CONSIDERATIONS

[§1.15] Representing Multiple Creditors

Former Cal Rules of Prof Cond 4–101 and 5–102 have been repealed. On the representation of adverse interests, now see Cal Rules of Prof Cond 3–310.

Attorneys' Fees

[§1.18] Contingent Fee Contracts

Business and Professions Code §6147(a)(6) now requires that contingency fee agreements disclose the attorney's failure to maintain errors and omissions insurance coverage or the failure to file a written guaranty agreement with the State Bar. Business and Professions Code §6148(a), governing noncontingency fee contracts, contains the same provision. These provisions remain in effect until January 1, 2000, unless a later enacted statute extends that date. Bus & P C §§6147–6148.

The requirements of Bus & P C §§6147–6148 do not apply to contingent fee contracts for the recovery of claims between merchants, as defined in Com C §2104, arising from the sale or lease of goods, services rendered, or money loaned for use in the conduct of a business or profession if the merchant contracting for legal services employs ten or more individuals. Bus & P C §6147.5. However, in the absence of a written contingent fee agreement, the attorney must limit his or her fees to the amounts specified in the statute. See Bus & P C §6147.5(b).

1 California Civil Procedure Before Trial §§1.7–1.24 (Cal CEB 1977) have been replaced by 1 California Civil Procedure Before Trial, chap 6 (3d ed Cal CEB 1990).

[§1.19] Arrangements Between Forwarder and Receiver

Former Cal Rules of Prof Cond 2–108(A) has been repealed and replaced by Cal Rules of Prof Cond 2–200(A), which provides:

> (A) A member shall not divide a fee for legal services with a lawyer who is not a partner of, associate of, or shareholder with the member unless:
>
> (1) The client has consented in writing thereto after a full disclosure has been made in writing that a division of fees will be made and the terms of such division; and
>
> (2) The total fee charged by all lawyers is not increased solely by reason of the provision for division of fees and is not unconscionable as that term is defined in Rule 4–200.

1 California Civil Procedure Before Trial §1.25 (Cal CEB 1977) has been replaced by 1 California Civil Procedure Before Trial §6.23 (3d ed Cal CEB 1990).

RECEIPT OF CLAIM

Assignment of Claim

[§1.25] Purpose of Assignment

The former Collection Agency Act (former Bus & P C §§6850–6956.1) and former 16 Cal Code Regs §§600–630, which implemented the Act, were repealed, effective June 30, 1992.

CONTACTING AND DEALING WITH DEBTOR

[§1.39] Sample Form: Reply to Letter From Debtor's Attorney

Former Cal Rules of Prof Cond 7–103 has been repealed. Now see Cal Rules of Prof Cond 2–100.

Procedure When Debtor Responds

[§1.41] Negotiation and Settlement

Civil Code §1526 clarifies the law regarding accord and satisfaction of disputed debts. When a debtor tenders a check as full payment of a disputed claim and words such as "payment in full" are written on the check, the creditor's acceptance of the check does not constitute an accord and satisfaction if the creditor protests against the tender as full payment by deleting the notation or if the acceptance of the check was inadvertent or without knowledge of the notation. CC §1526(a). Nonetheless, the creditor's acceptance of the check constitutes an accord and satisfaction when the check is issued under or in conjunction with a release of the claim. CC §1526(c). If certain specified conditions are met, acceptance of the check constitutes accord and satisfaction if the payment was tendered under a composition agreement between a debtor and its creditors. See CC §1526(b) and (d).

[§1.42] Confession of Judgment

Under 16 CFR §444.2, lenders or retail installment sellers may not take or receive a confession of judgment from consumers in connection with the extension of credit. In other words, confessions of judgment in contracts for consumer credit and installment sales are prohibited. This prohibition also extends to any waiver of the right to notice and the opportunity to be heard in the event of suit or process based on the transaction.

[§1.49] ADVISING CREDITORS ABOUT COLLECTION PRACTICES

The former Collection Agency Act (former Bus & P C §§6850–6956.1) and former 16 Cal Code Regs §§600–630, which implemented the Act, were repealed, effective June 30, 1992.

[§1.53] Defending Debt Collection Torts Claims

There is no cause of action for the malicious prosecution of an appeal. A party may not bring an action to recover damages for injury caused by a meritless appeal filed for delay, coercing settlement, or other improper purpose. *Coleman v Gulf Ins. Group* (1986) 41 C3d 782, 226 CR 90. The appropriate remedy for meritless appeals is found at CCP §907, authorizing an appellate court to assess damages for frivolous appeals.

[§1.56] Abuse of Process

A meritless appeal taken for delay or other improper purpose does not constitute abuse of process. Such conduct lacks an essential element of the tort, *i.e.,* the willful improper use of process. *Coleman v Gulf Ins. Group* (1986) 41 C3d 782, 226 CR 90. The *Coleman* court, however, noted that an aggrieved litigant may seek sanctions against a party under CCP §907 for a frivolous appeal. Under CCP §907, such sanctions are left to the discretion of the appellate court and cannot be recovered in a separate action.

1 California Civil Procedure Before Trial §9.20 (Cal CEB 1977) has been replaced by 2 California Civil Procedure Before Trial §30.19 (3d ed Cal CEB 1990).

[§1.57] Defending Fair Debt Collection Practices Act Suits

A collection agency was denied an award of attorney fees under 15 USC §1692k(a)(3) in *Juras v Aman Collection Serv.* (9th Cir 1987) 829 F2d 739. The court held that the debtor's conduct could not constitute bad faith under the statute when the debtor was unrepresented by counsel and was understandably confused by complex legal doctrine. In addition, there was no authority that the debtor's suit was clearly without merit at the time it was filed.

2

Representing the Debtor

[§2.1] SCOPE OF CHAPTER

1, 2 California Civil Procedure Before Trial (2d ed Cal CEB 1977, 1978) have been replaced by 1, 2, 3 California Civil Procedure Before Trial (3d ed Cal CEB 1990).

1, 2 California Civil Procedure During Trial (Cal CEB 1982, 1984) have been replaced by 1, 2, 3 California Trial Practice: Civil Procedure During Trial (3d ed Cal CEB 1995).

ANALYZING DEBTOR'S PROBLEM

[§2.10] Form: Debtor's Questionnaire

The debtor's questionnaire should be revised as follows to conform to corresponding changes in official bankruptcy forms:

15.b. (1) Have you paid any money or transferred any property to an attorney, to another person on behalf of an attorney, or to any person providing services to you relating to your financial affairs in the past year? Yes___ No___

15.c. (1) Have you agreed to pay any money or transfer any property to an attorney, to another person on behalf of an attorney, or to any person providing services to you relating to your financial affairs? Yes___ No___

16.i. Do you owe any debts to a farmer or fisherman? Yes___ No___

16.j. If your answer is yes, please identify and explain:

REPRESENTING DEBTORS

Consumer Debtors

[§2.19] Creditor's Attitude

Former Cal Rules of Prof Cond 7–104 has been repealed. Now see Cal Rules of Prof Cond 5–100.

[§2.20] Attorneys' Fees

The references in Book §2.20 to California Attorney's Fees Award Practice (Cal CEB 1982) should now be to California Attorney Fee Awards (2d ed Cal CEB 1994).

[§2.21] Use of Confession of Judgment Limited

On federal limitations on the use of confessions of judgment, see 16 CFR §444.2, discussed in Update §1.42.

[§2.24] Small Claims Court

Former CCP §§116–117.41 have been repealed. Small claims court actions are now governed by CCP §§116.110–116.950. Most of the substance of the former statutes has been retained by their replacements.

The jurisdictional maximum for small claims court is now $5000. CCP §116.220(a). However, the jurisdictional maximum for an action against a guarantor is $2500. CCP §116.220(c).

No person may file more than two small claims court actions in which the amount demanded exceeds $2500 anywhere in the state in any calendar year. If the amount demanded exceeds $2500, the party making the demand must file a declaration under penalty of perjury attesting to the fact that not more than two small claims court actions in which the amount of the demand exceeds $2500 have been filed by that party in the calendar year. CCP §116.231.

Under CCP §116.710, the plaintiff has no right to appeal a small claims court judgment. CCP §116.710(a). However, the defendant may appeal, and the plaintiff may appeal a judgment entered on the defendant's cross-complaint. CCP §116.710(b). Note that no party has a right to a jury trial on appeal to the superior court. CCP §116.770(b).

Code of Civil Procedure §116.140(b) provides that the attachment provisions of CCP §§481.010–481.225 do not apply in small claims court. Under CCP §116.820(a), a small claims court judgment can be enforced as provided in CCP §§680.010–724.260 and in CCP §§674 and 1174.

Under CCP §116.540(g), a defendant who is a nonresident owner of real property may defend against a claim relating to that property without personally appearing by (1) submitting written declarations as evidence in defense against the claim, or (2) having another person appear on his or her behalf if that person is serving without compensation and has appeared in small claims actions on behalf of others no more than four times during the calendar year, or both (1) and (2). Section 116.540(h) allows a party who is an owner of rental real property to appear and participate in actions involving that property through a property agent under contract with the owner to manage the rental of that property.

At the small claims court hearing, an individual appearing as a representative under subsections (g) or (h) must file a declaration stating that the individual is authorized to appear for the party and giving the basis for that authorization. CCP §116.540(i). If the representative is serving under subsection (g), the declaration must also state that the representative is serving without compensation and has appeared in small claims actions on behalf of others no more than four times during the calendar year. If the representative is serving under subsection (h), the declaration must also state that the representative is not employed solely to represent the party in small claims court.

In small claims proceedings, relevant hearsay evidence is admissible subject only to the law of testimonial privilege and a court's discretion under Evid C §352 to exclude unduly time-consuming, prejudicial, confusing, or misleading evidence. The trial court then exercises its sound discretion in determining the weight to which the evidence is entitled. *Houghtaling v Superior Court* (1993) 17 CA4th 1128, 21 CR2d 855. The court in *Houghtaling* reversed the trial court's refusal to consider the affidavit of an out-of-state witness.

Former Cal Rules of Ct 155 was repealed effective July 1, 1991. However, CCP §116.770(c) provides that attorneys may represent parties in appeals from small claims court judgments.

Married Persons

[§2.27] Separate Property

For purposes of creditors' rights, "quasi-community property" is treated as separate property. See California Marital Termination Agreements §3.21 (Cal CEB 1988).

[§2.30] Rescuing Debtor From Default Judgment

On the importance of *promptly* moving to obtain relief from default, see *Shamblin v Brattain* (1988) 44 C3d 474, 243 CR 902, discussed in Update §6.12.

Former CCP §117.8 has been repealed and replaced by CCP §116.730 without change material to the discussion in Book §2.30. For further discussion, see Update §6.13.

2 California Civil Procedure Before Trial, chap 30 (Cal CEB 1978) has been replaced by 3 California Civil Procedure Before Trial, chap 56 (3d ed Cal CEB 1990).

Dealing With Creditors

[§2.32] Consolidation Loans

Former 11 USC §522(f)(2), referred to in Book §2.32, has been renumbered §522(f)(1)(B).

ANALYZING CREDITOR-DEBTOR TRANSACTIONS

[§2.37] Contract Defenses

1 Witkin, Summary of California Law, *Contracts* (8th ed 1973) has been replaced by 1 Witkin, Summary of California Law, *Contracts* (9th ed 1987). Corbin on Contracts (1963) has been replaced by Corbin on Contracts (rev ed 1993) and Williston, Contracts (3d ed 1925) has been replaced by Williston, Contracts (4th ed 1990).

[§2.39] Unconscionability

Former CC §1770(s) has been redesignated as CC §1770(a)(19).

A 200-percent-per-year interest rate on a loan amount of $99,000 secured by a deed of trust was held unconscionable under CC §1670.5 in *Carboni v Arrospide* (1991) 2 CA4th 76, 2 CR2d 845. The court in *Carboni* disagreed with *Peoples Fin. & Thrift Co. v Mike-Ron Corp.* (1965) 236 CA2d 897, 46 CR 897, which suggested that interest rates were exempt from the unconscionability doctrine.

[§2.40] Void or Voidable Contract

Former CC §§25–42 have been repealed and replaced by CC §§38–41 and Fam C §§6500–6950, effective January 1, 1994.

Contracts That Violate Consumer Statutes or Regulations

Unfair or Deceptive Practices

[§2.45] Federal Law

See 16 CFR §§433.1–433.3 on required notices in consumer credit contracts.

Former 16 CFR Part 15 has been removed by the Federal Trade Commission to reduce the cost of publishing advisory opinions now considered to be of little value or available elsewhere.

Former 16 CFR §§14.2, 14.4, 14.7, 14.11, and 14.17 have been repealed and 16 CFR §14.16 was revised effective August 15, 1995. FTC standards for unfair or deceptive practices appear in 16 CFR Chap 1.

California Law

[§2.46] Unfair Competition; Bus & P C §§17200–17208

The Unfair Practices Act (Bus & P C §§17000–17101) and related enforcement measures under Bus & P C §§17200–17208 apply only to ongoing wrongful business conduct. The Act contemplates a pattern or course of conduct, not merely a single act or transaction. *State ex rel Van de Kamp v Texaco, Inc.* (1988) 46 C3d 1147, 1169, 252 CR 221, 235.

[§2.47] Consumers Legal Remedies Act

The Consumers Legal Remedies Act (CLRA) now lists 23 deceptive practices as actionable. Civil Code §§1770(a)(1)–(23) cover the following categories: (1) passing off goods or services as those of another (CC §1770(a)(1)); (2) misrepresenting goods or services (CC §1770(a)(2)–(8), (13)–(18)); (3) false or deceptive advertising (CC §1770(a)(9)–(12), (20)); and (4) unconscionable contract provisions (CC §1770(a)(19)).

A consumer may bring an action under the CLRA for restitution of property, as well as actual and punitive damages. CC §1780(a).

Civil Code §1770(a)(23) (former CC §1770(w)) prohibits home solicitation of a consumer who is a senior citizen when a loan is made encumbering the primary residence of the consumer for the purposes of paying for home improvements and the transaction is part of a pattern or practice in violation of provisions of federal law.

Effective January 1, 1997, CC §1770(b) makes it an unfair or deceptive act or practice for a mortgage broker or lender to use a home improvement contractor to negotiate the terms of any loan used to finance a home improvement contract that is secured by the borrower's residence.

Credit and Installment Sales

Federal Law

[§§2.50–2.56] Truth in Lending; Attorneys' Fees

For a recent case interpreting whether a loan was a "consumer credit transaction" subject to the Truth in Lending Act, see *Weber v Langholz* (1995) 39 CA4th 1578, 46 CR2d 677. In *Weber*, a loan made to an individual as trustee of her revocable living trust was not a consumer loan because 15 USC §1603(*l*) exempts extensions of credit to "organizations," and the definition of organization in 15 USC §1602(c) includes a trust. The loan also failed to qualify as one for "personal, family, or household purposes" under 15 USC §1602(h) because it was undisputed that it was used to fund an investment in coins. On this point, the court relied on *Thorns v Sundance Prop.* (9th Cir 1984) 726 F2d 1417.

An action to enforce a violation of the Truth in Lending Act may now be brought by the state attorney general in any state court or United States district court. 15 USC §1640(e). Title 15 USC §1640(a) has also been amended to provide that, in the case of failure to comply with any requirement under 15 USC §1639, in addition to the other damages provided for, damages shall include an amount equal to the sum of all finance charges and fees paid by the consumer, unless the creditor demonstrates that the failure to comply was not material. 15 USC §1640(a)(4).

Former 15 USC §1603(6), cited in Book §2.52, has been redesignated as 15 USC §1603(7).

[§2.59] California Credit Protection Laws

Consumer credit transactions involving cosigners are now governed by CC §§1799.90–1799.103.

Effective July 1, 1995, the Personal Property Brokers Law (former Fin C §§22000–22654), the Consumer Finance Lenders Law (former Fin C §§24000–24654), and the Commercial Finance Lenders Law (former Fin C §§26000–26653) were consolidated and renamed the California Finance Lenders Law in Fin C §§22000–22780.

[§2.63] Penalties; Opportunity To Correct Violations

Effective July 1, 1995, the Personal Property Brokers Law (former Fin C §§22000–22654), the Consumer Finance Lenders Law (former Fin C §§24000–24654), and the Commercial Finance Lenders Law (former Fin C §§26000–26653) were consolidated and renamed the California Finance Lenders Law in Fin C §§22000–22780. Remedies for violations of the California Finance Lenders Law are found at Fin C §§22700–22780.

[§2.65] Repossession and Resale

The following cases were cited incorrectly in Book §2.65: *Culbertson v Leland* (9th Cir 1975) 528 F2d 426; *Nicholas v Harger-Haldeman* (1961) 196 CA2d 77, 16 CR 195. These are their correct citations.

Business and Professions Code §7507.9(h) allows a debtor to waive the preparation of an inventory when the debtor redeems personal property not subject to the security interest and signs a specified statement. Effective January 1, 1997, Bus & P C §7507.9(i) allows a repossession agency to request written authorization from the debtor or the legal owner to release personal property not covered by a security interest to someone other than the debtor.

[§2.66] Action on Bond

Former Bus & P C §7398 has been repealed. There now is apparently no requirement that cosmetology schools post a bond.

Interest and Finance Charges

Computing and Quoting Finance Charges

[§2.71] California Law

Effective July 1, 1995, the Personal Property Brokers Law (former Fin C §§22000–22654), the Consumer Finance Lenders Law (former Fin C §§24000–24654), and the Commercial Finance Lenders Law (former Fin C §§26000–26653) were consolidated and renamed the California Finance Lenders Law in Fin C §§22000–22780. The maximum rates found in former Fin C §22451 are now found in Fin C §22303. The precompute method described in Book §2.71 under former Fin C §22480 is now in Fin C §22400.

[§2.73] California Consumer Loan Regulation

Effective July 1, 1995, consumer finance companies that operated under the Personal Property Brokers Law (former Fin C §§22000–22654) or the Consumer Finance Lenders Law (former Fin C §§24000–24654) will be governed by the California Finance Lenders Law (former Fin C §§22000–22780). See §§2.74–2.75.

The correct citation for administrative regulations governing mortgage loan brokers is 10 Cal Code Regs §§2840–2849.1.

California Real Property Sales Transactions §2.3 (Cal CEB 1981) has been replaced by California Real Property Sales Transactions §2.5 (2d ed Cal CEB 1993).

[§2.74] Personal Property Brokers Law

Effective July 1, 1995, the Personal Property Brokers Law (former

Fin C §§22000–22654), the Consumer Finance Lenders Law (former Fin C §§24000–24654), and the Commercial Finance Lenders Law (former Fin C §§26000–26653) were consolidated and renamed the California Finance Lenders Law in Fin C §§22000–22780.

The correct citation for administrative regulations governing personal property brokers is 10 Cal Code Regs §§1404–1570.

[§2.75] Consumer Finance Lenders Law

Effective July 1, 1995, the Personal Property Brokers Law (former Fin C §§22000–22654), the Consumer Finance Lenders Law (former Fin C §§24000–24654), and the Commercial Finance Lenders Law (former Fin C §§26000–26653) were consolidated and renamed the California Finance Lenders Law in Fin C §§22000–22780.

The correct citation for administrative regulations governing consumer finance lenders, commercial finance lenders, and personal property brokers is 10 Cal Code Regs §§1404–1570.

[§§2.78–2.79] Finance Charges in Retail Installment Sales

Civil Code §1805.1 bars annual fees or charges in any retail installment contract. However, other fees and charges are permissible under the statute. See also CC §1803.3.

Former CC §1808.6 has been repealed. Stats 1991, ch 819.

[§§2.80–2.81] Retail Installment Accounts; Methods of Calculation

Civil Code §1810.2 has been amended to provide that the seller or holder of a retail installment account may charge, receive, and collect a finance charge as disclosed to the buyer under CC §1810.3. Any change in the finance charge is effective only with respect to purchases made on or after the effective date of the change and is not effective until the seller has given notice of the change. CC §1810.4.

[§§2.84–2.92] Usury

A provision in a commercial sales contract calling for interest charges on late payments is not subject to the usury law. *Southwest Concrete Prods. v Gosh Constr. Corp.* (1990) 51 C3d 701, 274 CR 404. The court reasoned that such charges are not usurious because they do not constitute payment for the loan or forbearance of money. As a form of seller financing for the purchase of property, the charges fall under the "time-price" exception to the usury law and the principle that a debtor by voluntary act may not render an otherwise valid contract usurious. The court explicitly disapproved *Crestwood Lumber Co. v Citizens Sav. & Loan Ass'n* (1978) 83 CA3d 819, 148 CR 129, and *Mark McDowell Corp. v LSM 128* (1989) 214 CA3d 1427, 263 CR 310, both of which held to the contrary.

There is no violation of the usury laws when a seller of real property, by agreement of the parties, increases the interest rate on a secured purchase money promissory note from 10 percent to 15 percent in exchange for an extension of the due date of the note. The original transaction was a credit sale and therefore exempt from the usury laws. The exempt status was retained even when the interest rate was modified. *DCM Partners v Smith* (1991) 228 CA3d 729, 737, 278 CR 778, 782. See also *Ghirardo v Antonioli* (1994) 8 C4th 791, 35 CR2d 418.

Parties to a loan agreement may anticipate the possibility of default and provide in the loan agreement that accrued interest will itself bear interest. To be enforceable, such a provision must be explicit in the agreement. *Ninety Five Ten v Crain* (1991) 231 CA3d 36, 282 CR 141.

If a contract entered into after January 1, 1986, does not stipulate a legal rate of interest, the obligation bears interest at 10 percent per year after a breach. CC §3289(b). If an interest provision in a contract entered into after January 1, 1986, is void because it is usurious, the injured party is entitled to prejudgment interest at 10 percent per year as prescribed by CC §3289(b). *Mark McDowell Corp. v LSM 128, supra.* This aspect of the decision in *Mark McDowell* was not overruled by the supreme court in *Southwest Concrete Prods. v Gosh Constr. Corp., supra.* This holding is also consistent with *Epstein v Frank* (1981) 125 CA3d 111, 177 CR 831, discussed in Book §2.86.

For examples of cases in which loans arranged by brokers were held exempt from usury limitations under CC §1916.1, see *Jones v Kallman* (1988) 199 CA3d 131, 244 CR 609, and *Stickel v Harris* (1987) 196 CA3d 575, 242 CR 88.

For an application of the unconscionability doctrine to high interest rates, see *Carboni v Arrospide* (1991) 2 CA4th 76, 2 CR2d 845, discussed in Update §2.39.

For an extensive discussion of usury, see Rabin & Brownlie, *Usury Law in California: A Guide Through the Maze*, 20 UC Davis L Rev 397 (Spring 1987).

The discussion of 12 USC §86a in Book §2.85 is misleading. The text should say that 12 USC §86a preempts state law regarding business or agricultural loans over $1000 when state usury limits are lower than the prescribed rate in §86a. Section 86a applied only to this category of loans made between April 1, 1980, and April 1, 1983, or until the date on which a state adopted a law explicitly providing that §86a did not apply.

False Advertising

Remedies Under State Law

[§2.99] Advertising Mail-Order Businesses

Business and Professions Code §17538.5 was amended effective January 1, 1995 to cover businesses using private mail box receiving services.

[§2.101] Civil Penalty and Injunction

Former Bus & P C §17536(b) has been redesignated Bus & P C §17536(c). Under current Bus & P C §17536(b), the court must impose a civil penalty for each violation under Bus & P C §§17500–17581.

Private litigants may not recover compensatory damages under the enforcement provisions of the Unfair Practices Act (see Bus & P C §§17200–17209). *Bank of the West v Superior Court* (1992) 2 C4th 1254, 1273, 10 CR2d 538, 551. In *Bank of the West*, the supreme court disapproved *UFW v Superior Court,* cited in Book §2.101.

Breach of Warranty

Song-Beverly Consumer Warranty Act

[§§2.104–2.105] Service and Repair

Consumers should note amendments to CC §1793.2 that entitle the purchaser of a motor vehicle to a replacement or to restitution if the manufacturer or its representative is unable to service or repair the vehicle after a reasonable number of attempts. CC §1793.2(d)(2). See also *Bishop v Hyundai Motor America* (1996) 44 CA4th 750, 52 CR2d 134; *Jensen v BMW of N. Am., Inc.* (1995) 35 CA4th 112, 41 CR2d 295; *Schreidel v American Honda Motor Co., Inc.* (1995) 34 CA4th 1242, 40 CR2d 576; *National R.V., Inc. v Foreman* (1995) 34 CA4th 1072, 40 CR2d 672.

Fraud

[§2.108] Statutory Definition; Elements

California Real Property Sales Transactions §§2.86–2.102 (Cal CEB 1981) have been replaced by California Real Property Sales Transactions §§2.99–2.132 (2d ed Cal CEB 1993).

[§2.111] Sample Form: Complaint for Damages for Fraud and Violation of Finance Lenders [Formerly Personal Property Brokers] Law

Effective July 1, 1995, the Personal Property Brokers Law (former Fin C §§22000–22654), the Consumer Finance Lenders Law (former Fin

C §§24000–24654), and the Commercial Finance Lenders Law (former Fin C §§26000–26653) were consolidated and renamed the California Finance Lenders Law in Fin C §§22000–22780. Accordingly, if an action is brought on a loan made after July 1, 1995, the complaint should be recaptioned "Complaint for Damages for Fraud and Violation of Finance Lenders Law (Fin C §§22000–22780)."

The citation for administrative regulations governing personal property brokers in paragraph 13 of the form should be to 10 Cal Code Regs §§1404–1570.

James v Public Fin. Corp. (1975) 47 CA3d 995, 121 CR2d 670, cited in Book §2.11, was criticized in *Cheung v Daley* (1995) 35 CA4th 1673, 42 CR2d 164, which declined to read a punitive damages award as a combined award with a compensatory damages element and held that any award of exemplary damages must be accompanied by an express award of compensatory damages.

[§2.112] COLLECTION ABUSES

The former Collection Agency Act (former Bus & P C §§6850–6956.1) and former 16 Cal Code Regs §§600–630, which implemented the Act, were repealed, effective June 30, 1992.

Statutory Regulation of Collectors

[§§2.115–2.116] California Collection Agency Act

The former Collection Agency Act (former Bus & P C §§6850–6956.1) and former 16 Cal Code Regs §§600–630, which implemented the Act, were repealed, effective June 30, 1992.

Federal and California Fair Debt Collection Practices Acts

[§2.119] Preemption

Debt Collection Manual, cited in the Book, has been replaced by Collection Agency Laws, Rules, and Regulations. Sacramento, Calif.: Bureau of Collection and Investigative Services (1982).

[§2.120] Enforcement

The former Collection Agency Act (former Bus & P C §§6850–6956.1) and former 16 Cal Code Regs §§600–630, which implemented the Act, were repealed, effective June 30, 1992.

[§2.121] Prohibited Practices

The former Collection Agency Act (former Bus & P C §§6850–6956.1) and former 16 Cal Code Regs §§600–630, which implemented the Act, were repealed, effective June 30, 1992.

For an example of actionable conduct under 15 USC §1692e, see *Juras v Aman Collection Serv.* (9th Cir 1987) 829 F2d 739 (misleading statements in letters).

Collection Torts

[§2.127] Sample Allegation Form: Invasion of Privacy

The Consumer Credit Reporting Agencies Act (CC §§1785.1–1785.35) limits actions for invasion of privacy against agencies subject to the Act. Under CC §1785.32, a credit reporting agency cannot be liable for invasion of privacy unless "the reporting agency, with malice, collects, stores or disseminates false information concerning the consumer." *Hiemstra v Crocker Nat'l Bank* (1987) 195 CA3d 1629, 1635, 241 CR 564, 567.

[§2.135] Class Actions

The correct citation for *Fletcher v Security Pac. Nat'l Bank,* cited in Book §2.135, is *Fletcher v Security Pac. Nat'l Bank* (1979) 23 C3d 442, 153 CR 28. See also *Dean Witter Reynolds, Inc. v Superior Court* (1989) 211 CA3d 758, 259 CR 759.

3

Filing Debt Collection Actions

[§3.1] CHECKLIST: SHOULD COLLECTION ACTION BE FILED?

1, 2 California Civil Procedure Before Trial (2d ed Cal CEB 1977, 1978) have been replaced by 1, 2, 3 California Civil Procedure Before Trial (3d ed Cal CEB 1990).

JURISDICTION AND VENUE

[§3.2] Subject Matter Jurisdiction

Collection cases filed in superior court will be subject to the Trial Court Delay Reduction Act (Govt C §§68600–68620), which is in effect in all superior courts in California. Municipal and justice courts have also established delay reduction programs consistent with the Act. Govt C §68620. Counsel should check applicable local rules. For further discussion, see Update §1.1.

Former CCP §§116–117.41 have been repealed. Small claims actions are now governed by CCP §§116.110–116.950. The jurisdictional maximum for small claims court has increased to $5000. CCP §116.220(a). However, the demand in a small claims action against a guarantor may not exceed $2500. CCP §116.220(c). Under CCP §116.220(a)(4) the small claims court has jurisdiction to confirm, correct, or vacate a binding fee arbitration award not exceeding $5000 between an attorney and a client, or to conduct a hearing de novo after nonbinding arbitration of a fee dispute involving no more than $5000 under Bus & P C §§6200–6206.

No person may file more than two small claims actions in which the amount demanded exceeds $2500, anywhere in the state in any calendar year. If the amount demanded in a small claims action exceeds $2500, the party making the demand must file a declaration under penalty of perjury attesting to the fact that not more than two small claims actions in which the amount of the demand exceeds $2500 have been filed by that party in the calendar year. CCP §116.231.

Former CCP §117.5 has been replaced by CCP §116.420, which continues to bar an assignee of a claim from filing or maintaining a claim in small claims court.

For further discussion of current small claims court procedures, see Update §2.24.

1 California Civil Procedure Before Trial §§2.3–2.19 (Cal CEB 1977) have been replaced by 1 California Civil Procedure Before Trial §§13.3–13.17 (3d ed Cal CEB 1990).

[§3.3] Amount Demanded in Prayer Governs

The reference to CCP §1033 in the last line of the second paragraph in the Book should be changed to CCP §1033(a).

Under CCP §396, a superior court case must be transferred to municipal court (1) when the absence of jurisdiction is apparent before trial from the complaint, petition, or related documents, or (2) when it becomes apparent before trial that a matter will *necessarily* result in a verdict below the superior court jurisdictional limit. The superior court must give the parties an opportunity to contest the proposed transfer. *Walker v Superior Court* (1991) 53 C3d 257, 262, 279 CR 576, 578. Elaborating on what is meant by requiring that a matter "necessarily" result in a verdict below the jurisdictional limit, the supreme court stated that this requires a high level of certainty that a damage award will not exceed the municipal court jurisdictional maximum. This requirement is not satisfied by a finding that such an award is merely "unlikely" or "not reasonably probable." 53 C3d at 269. The court also provided a number of guidelines to assist courts in the application of CCP §396. First, when considering a transfer under the statute, a court should proceed by noticed motion. At the very least, once the jurisdictional issue is raised, the parties must have an opportunity to respond and offer reasons why transfer should or should not be ordered. A court must exercise caution to ensure that information from settlement negotiations is not improperly divulged in the context of a transfer hearing. Trial courts must avoid using the transfer power as a way of clearing crowded court calendars, and should use the transfer power sparingly. The supreme court also noted the importance of making a record of the transfer hearing to facilitate appellate review. 53 C3d at 271.

Code of Civil Procedure §1033 has been amended to limit the recovery of costs in a municipal or justice court action when the plaintiff recovers less than the jurisdictional limit of the small claims court. When the action could have been brought in small claims court, the court has discretion to allow or deny all or part of the plaintiff's costs. CCP §1033(b)(1). When the action could not have been brought in small claims court, recoverable costs are limited to the actual filing fees, the actual cost of service of process, and when otherwise specifically allowed by law, reasonable attorney fees. However, these costs are recoverable only if, before the action began, the plaintiff informed the defendant in writing of both the intended legal action and the possibility that a judgment could include such costs. CCP §1033(b)(2).

[§3.4] Waiver of Excess Amount

Yousafzai v Hyundai Motor Am. (1994) 22 CA4th 920, 27 CR2d 569, holds that a writ of mandate under CCP §400, rather than an appeal, must be used to obtain review of an order of transfer under CCP §396 when transfer is based on evaluation of the amount recoverable in the action. See also *Ash v Hertz Corp.* (1997) 53 CA4th 1107, 62 CR2d 192, distinguishing *Yousafzai* and holding that when a motion is made to transfer a municipal court case to superior court on the ground that the amount in controversy exceeds the municipal court's jurisdiction and that motion is denied, the party aggrieved may obtain appellate review on appeal from the final judgment entered by the municipal court.

[§3.5] Multiple Parties and Claims

1 California Civil Procedure Before Trial §§7.6, 7.12–7.15 (Cal CEB 1977) have been replaced by 1 California Civil Procedure Before Trial §§21.7–21.11 (3d ed Cal CEB 1990).

Venue

[§3.7] Legal Requirements; Tactical Considerations

Code of Civil Procedure §395(b) has been amended to specify venue in actions based on the "offer or provision," of goods, services, loans, or extensions of credit intended primarily for personal, family, or household use. It also provides for venue in actions arising from a transaction consummated as a proximate result of an unsolicited telephone call made by a seller engaged in the business of consummating transactions of that kind. Trial of the action is proper in the county where the buyer/lessee signed the contract, the county where the buyer/lessee resided when the contract was signed, or the county where the buyer/lessee resides when the action is commenced.

1 California Civil Procedure Before Trial, chap 3 (Cal CEB 1977) has been replaced by 2 California Civil Procedure Before Trial, chap 28 (3d ed Cal CEB 1990).

Requirements

[§3.9] In Specific Situations

Unincorporated associations: When an unincorporated association is joined along with individual defendants, venue is proper at the residence of any individual defendant even if the association has filed a statement designating a principal office under Corp C §24003, as authorized by CCP §395.2. This is the same rule that applies to corporations and individuals named as defendants. The individual must be a legitimate defendant and not be named to manipulate venue. *Buran Equip. Co. v Superior Court* (1987) 190 CA3d 1662, 236 CR 171.

THE COMPLAINT

[§3.11] Tactical Considerations

1 California Civil Procedure Before Trial, chap 7 (Cal CEB 1977) has been replaced by 1 California Civil Procedure Before Trial, chap 22 (3d ed Cal CEB 1990).

Common Counts

[§§3.14–3.15] Book Account; Account Stated

For a case applying criteria for determining whether a book account exists or whether there is an account stated between the parties, see *Maggio, Inc. v Neal* (1987) 196 CA3d 745, 241 CR 883.

On the recovery of attorney fees when an action on a contract is based on a book account, see CC §1717.5, discussed in Update §6.41.

[§3.20] Statute of Limitations

Ordinarily, the statute of limitations on a book account begins to run on the last entry in the account. See Book §3.20. However, in *R.N.C., Inc. v Tsegeletos* (1991) 231 CA3d 967, 283 CR 48, the court stated that any payment toward the debt is not necessarily an "entry" for purposes of the limitations period. The court held that a book account closes and the statute of limitations begins to run once the account creditor stops extending credit and there is no further activity on the account other than payments credited towards the settled debt. Thus, when the creditor in *Tsegeletos* demanded full payment of the account's outstanding balance and refused to extend further credit, the account closed and the statute began to run. Payments made by the debtor after that time were merely partial payments towards a fixed debt and did not serve to reopen the account. Although the court failed to discuss the issue at length, it refused to accept without qualification the statement in *Furlow Pressed Brick Co. v Balboa Land & Water Co.* (1921) 186 C 754, 200 P 625, cited in Book §3.20, that a debtor's subsequent payment and the creditor's resulting entry in the account toll the statute of limitations.

Basic Complaint Forms

[§3.25] Form: Basic Collection Complaint With Common Count Charging Allegations

1 California Civil Procedure Before Trial, chap 7 (Cal CEB 1977) has been replaced by 1 California Civil Procedure Before Trial, chap 22 (3d ed Cal CEB 1990).

Complaint Form Provisions for Specific Allegations

[§3.30] Form: Complaint on Judgment

Comment: California's statutory limitation on the recovery of attorney fees incurred in the enforcement of a judgment (CCP §685.040) does not apply to a sister-state judgment awarding such fees. The award of fees in a sister-state judgment is enforceable under the full faith and credit clause. *Aspen Int'l Capital Corp. v Marsch* (1991) 235 CA3d 1199, 286 CR 921.

[§3.31] Form: Recovery of Deficiency Balance

Comment: No written notice of intention to sell a motor vehicle under CC §2983.2 is required when the vehicle has been seized by a federal, state, or local public agency or authority as described in CC §2983.3(b)(6). Other creditors must provide at least 15 days' written notice of intent to dispose of a repossessed vehicle. CC §2983.2(a). Effective January 1, 1997, CC §2983.2(a)(9) requires the notice of intent to dispose of a repossessed vehicle to inform the recipients that they will be liable for the deficiency balance plus interest at the contract rate, or at the legal rate of interest if there is no contract rate, from the date of disposition to the date of entry of judgment. Also effective January 1, 1997, CC §2983.35(b) provides that a creditor who fails to comply with that section may not recover from a cosigner the costs associated with recovery of the vehicle.

When a debtor defaults on a conditional sales contract and the creditor purchases the collateral at a foreclosure sale that does not comply with the notice provisions of Com C §9504, the creditor is not barred from obtaining a deficiency judgment if the collateral is repurchased at a new, properly noticed sale and there is no showing of prejudice to the debtor. *PWS, Inc. v Ban* (1991) 234 CA3d 223, 285 CR 598. For a recent case dealing with duties under Com C §9504, see *Ford & Vlahos v ITT Commercial Fin. Corp.* (1994) 8 C4th 1220, 36 CR2d 464.

[§3.36] Filing the Complaint

1 California Civil Procedure Before Trial, chap 7 (Cal CEB 1977) has been replaced in relevant part by 1 California Civil Procedure Before Trial, chaps 1, 22 (3d ed Cal CEB 1990).

SERVICE OF PROCESS

[§3.37] Checklist: Service of Process

Former Govt C §§27820–27829, dealing with constables, have been repealed. The reference to constables in Govt C §26665 has also been deleted.

1 California Civil Procedure Before Trial, chap 8 (Cal CEB 1977) has been replaced by 1 California Civil Procedure Before Trial, chap 24 (3d ed Cal CEB 1990).

II. MANNER OF SERVICE
A. Service Within California

3. Substituted service on natural person, minor, incompetent, or candidate for public office. Code of Civil Procedure §415.20(b) has been amended to authorize service at a person's usual mailing address other than a United States Postal Service post office box.

V. PROOF OF SERVICE
A. Service on Person Within California

1. Personal or substituted service. Code of Civil Procedure §417.10 has been amended to require that all proof of personal service be made on a form adopted by the Judicial Council. CCP §417.10(f).

[§3.38] Purpose

1 California Civil Procedure Before Trial, chap 2 (Cal CEB 1977) has been replaced by 1 California Civil Procedure Before Trial, chaps 13–14 (3d ed Cal CEB 1990).

1 California Civil Procedure Before Trial, chap 8 (Cal CEB 1977) has been replaced by 1 California Civil Procedure Before Trial, chap 24 (3d ed Cal CEB 1990).

California State Sheriffs' Association Civil Procedure Manual (3d ed rev 1978) has been replaced by California State Sheriffs' Association Civil Procedure Manual (4th ed rev 1994).

Summons Forms

[§3.39] Judicial Council Form 982(a)(9): Summons

Comment: Code of Civil Procedure §417.10(f) requires that all proof of personal service be made on a form adopted by the Judicial Council. The Judicial Council has approved an alternative proof of service (summons) form in addition to the one found on the reverse side of the summons form printed in Book §3.39. A copy of this alternative form is printed in Update §3.42.

[§3.41] Judicial Council Form 982(a)(4): Notice and Acknowledgment of Receipt

1 California Civil Procedure Before Trial §8.38 (2d ed Cal CEB 1977) has been replaced by 1 California Civil Procedure Before Trial §24.32 (3d ed Cal CEB 1990).

[§3.42] Judicial Council Form: Proof of Service

The reference in Book §3.42 to Book §9.39 should be to §3.39.

The Judicial Council has approved an alternative proof of service (summons) form in addition to the one found on the reverse side of the summons form printed in Book §3.39. A copy of this alternative form is printed on the following page.

ATTORNEY OR PARTY WITHOUT ATTORNEY *(Name and Address)*:	TELEPHONE NO.	FOR COURT USE ONLY
ATTORNEY FOR *(Name)*:	Ref. No. or File No.	
Insert name of court and name of judicial district and branch court, if any:		
SHORT TITLE OF CASE:		

PROOF OF SERVICE (Summons)	DATE:	TIME:	DEPT./DIV.:	CASE NUMBER:

1. At the time of service I was at least 18 years of age and not a party to this action, and **I served copies** of the *(specify documents)*:

2. a. Party served *(specify name of party as shown on the documents served)*:

   b. Person served: ☐ party in item 2a ☐ other *(specify name and title or relationship to the party named in item 2a)*:

   c. Address:

3. I served the party named in item 2
   a. ☐ **by personally delivering** the copies (1) on *(date)*: (2) at *(time)*:
   b. ☐ **by leaving** the copies with or in the presence of *(name and title or relationship to person indicated in item 2b)*:
      (1) ☐ **(business)** a person at least 18 years of age apparently in charge at the office or usual place of business of the person served. I informed him or her of the general nature of the papers.
      (2) ☐ **(home)** a competent member of the household (at least 18 years of age) at the dwelling house or usual place of abode of the person served. I informed him or her of the general nature of the papers.
      (3) on *(date)*: (4) at *(time)*:
      (5) ☐ A **declaration of diligence** is attached. *(Substituted service on natural person, minor, conservatee, or candidate.)*
   c. ☐ **by mailing** the copies to the person served, addressed as shown in item 2c, by first-class mail, postage prepaid,
      (1) on *(date)*: (2) from *(city)*:
      (3) ☐ with two copies of the Notice and Acknowledgment of Receipt and a postage-paid return envelope addressed to me.
      (4) ☐ to an address outside California with return receipt requested. *(Attach completed form.)*
   d. ☐ by causing copies to be mailed. A declaration of mailing is attached.
   e. ☐ **other** *(specify other manner of service and authorizing code section)*:
4. The "Notice to the Person Served" (on the summons) was completed as follows:
   a. ☐ as an individual defendant.
   b. ☐ as the person sued under the fictitious name of *(specify)*:
   c. ☐ on behalf of *(specify)*:
      under: ☐ CCP 416.10 (corporation) ☐ CCP 416.60 (minor) ☐ other:
      ☐ CCP 416.20 (defunct corporation) ☐ CCP 416.70 (conservatee)
      ☐ CCP 416.40 (association or partnership) ☐ CCP 416.90 (individual)
5. **Person serving** *(name, address, and telephone No.)*:
   a. **Fee** for service: $
   b. ☐ Not a registered California process server.
   c. ☐ Exempt from registration under B&P § 22350(b).
   d. ☐ Registered California process server.
      (1) ☐ Employee or independent contractor.
      (2) Registration No.:
      (3) County:
6. ☐ **I declare** under penalty of perjury under the laws of the State of California that the foregoing is true and correct.
7. ☐ **I am a California sheriff, marshal, or constable and** I certify that the foregoing is true and correct.

Date: ▶ (SIGNATURE)

Form Adopted by Rule 982
Judicial Council of California
982(a)(23) [New July 1, 1987]

PROOF OF SERVICE
(Summons)

Code Civ. Proc., § 417.10(f)

Comment: Code of Civil Procedure §417.10(f) requires that all proof of personal service be made on a form adopted by the Judicial Council. The form printed above is substantially the same as the proof of service portion of the form printed in Book §3.39.

Motion To Quash Service of Summons

[§§3.43–3.44] Procedure; Form: Notice of Motion To Quash Service of Summons

The notice of motion to quash service of summons must designate, as the time for making the motion, a date not more than 30 days after filing of the notice. The notice must be served in the manner and at the times prescribed by CCP §1005(b), which governs the timing of motions generally. CCP §§418.10, 1005(a)(4). For discussion of the requirements of CCP §1005(b), see Update §4.24.

Former CCP §904.1(c) has been redesignated CCP §904.1(a)(3).

1 California Civil Procedure Before Trial, chap 2 (Cal CEB 1977) has been replaced by 2 California Civil Procedure Before Trial, chap 27 (3d ed Cal CEB 1990).

[§3.46] Form: Order Quashing Service of Summons

Former CCP §904.1(c) has been redesignated CCP §904.1(a)(3).

DEBTOR'S RESPONSIVE PLEADINGS

[§3.49] Judicial Arbitration

Code of Civil Procedure §1141.11(a) and Cal Rules of Ct 1600 have been amended. The jurisdictional maximum for mandatory judicial arbitration is now $50,000.

2 California Civil Procedure Before Trial, chap 26A (Cal CEB 1978) has been replaced by 3 California Civil Procedure Before Trial, chap 55 (3d ed Cal CEB 1990).

[§3.50] Motion To Strike

A motion to strike may be filed after a motion for judgment on the pleadings has been granted with leave to amend, when the moving party contends that an amended pleading was filed too late or that the pleading violates the court's prior ruling on the motion. CCP §435(b)(1), (e); CCP §438(i)(1)(A).

1 California Civil Procedure Before Trial §10.1 (Cal CEB 1977) has been replaced by 2 California Civil Procedure Before Trial §31.2 (3d ed Cal CEB 1990).

[§3.51] Demurrer

1 California Civil Procedure Before Trial, chap 9 (Cal CEB 1977) has been replaced by 2 California Civil Procedure Before Trial, chap 30 (3d ed Cal CEB 1990).

Answer

[§3.60] Denial of Amount Claimed

1 California Civil Procedure Before Trial §11.2 (Cal CEB 1977) has been replaced by 2 California Civil Procedure Before Trial §32.19 (3d ed Cal CEB 1990).

General Denials

[§3.63] Judicial Council Form 982(a)(13): General Denial

ATTORNEY OR PARTY WITHOUT ATTORNEY *(Name and Address)*: TELEPHONE NO.:	*FOR COURT USE ONLY*
ATTORNEY FOR *(Name)*:	
Insert name of court, name of judicial district, and branch court, if any:	
PLAINTIFF:	
DEFENDANT:	
GENERAL DENIAL	CASE NUMBER:

You MUST use this form for your general denial if the amount asked for in the complaint or the value of the property involved is $1000 or less.

You MAY use this form if:
1. The complaint is not verified, OR
2. The complaint is verified, and the action is subject to the economic litigation procedures of the municipal and justice courts, EXCEPT

You MAY NOT use this form if the complaint is verified and involves a claim for more than $1000 that has been assigned to a third party for collection.

(See Code of Civil Procedure sections 90–100, 431.30, and 431.40.)

1. DEFENDANT *(name)*:
generally denies each and every allegation of plaintiff's complaint.

2. ☐ DEFENDANT states the following FACTS as separate affirmative defenses to plaintiff's complaint *(attach additional pages if necessary)*:

Date:

.... (TYPE OR PRINT NAME) ▶ ______________________ (SIGNATURE OF DEFENDANT OR ATTORNEY)

If you have a claim for damages or other relief against the plaintiff, the law may require you to state your claim in a special pleading called a cross-complaint or you may lose your claim. (See Code of Civil Procedure sections 426.10–426.40.)

The original of this General Denial must be filed with the clerk of this court with proof that a copy was served on each plaintiff's attorney and on each plaintiff not represented by an attorney. *(See the other side for a proof of service.)*

Form Adopted by Rule 982
Judicial Council of California
982(a)(13) [Rev. January 1, 1987]

GENERAL DENIAL

CCP 431.30, 431.40

PLAINTIFF *(name)*:	CASE NUMBER:
DEFENDANT *(name)*:	

PROOF OF SERVICE

☐ **Personal Service** ☐ **Mail**

A General Denial may be served by anyone at least 18 years of age EXCEPT you or any other party to this legal action. Service is made in one of the following ways:
(1) Personally delivering a copy to the attorney for the other party or, if no attorney, to the other party.
OR
(2) Mailing a copy, postage prepaid, to the last known address of the attorney for the other party or, if no attorney, to the other party.
Be sure whoever serves the General Denial fills out and signs a proof of service. File the proof of service with the court as soon as the General Denial is served.

1. At the time of service I was at least 18 years of age and **not a party to this legal action.**

2. I served a copy of the General Denial as follows *(check either a or b)*:

a. ☐ **Personal service.** I personally delivered the General Denial as follows:
(1) Name of person served:
(2) Address where served:

(3) Date served:
(4) Time served:

b. ☐ **Mail.** I deposited the General Denial in the United States mail, in a sealed envelope with postage fully prepaid. The envelope was addressed and mailed as follows:
(1) Name of person served:
(2) Address:

(3) Date of mailing:
(4) Place of mailing *(city and state)*:
(5) I am a resident of or employed in the county where the General Denial was mailed.

c. My residence or business address is *(specify)*:

d. My phone number is *(specify)*:

I declare under penalty of perjury under the laws of the State of California that the foregoing is true and correct.

Date:

(TYPE OR PRINT NAME OF PERSON WHO SERVED THE GENERAL DENIAL) ▶ (SIGNATURE OF PERSON WHO SERVED THE GENERAL DENIAL)

982(a)(13) (Rev. January 1, 1987) **GENERAL DENIAL** **(Proof of Service)** Page two

Comment: The Judicial Council has approved a revised form of general denial. The new form describes when its use is appropriate and emphasizes more strongly than its predecessor that defendants must state facts for affirmative defenses.

[§3.64] Affirmative Defenses

1 California Civil Procedure Before Trial §§11.19–11.31 (Cal CEB 1977) have been replaced by 2 California Civil Procedure Before Trial §§32.25–32.53 (3d ed Cal CEB 1990).

[§3.67] Statute of Limitations

Under CCP §360.5, a written waiver of a statute of limitations defense executed before the running of the applicable statute of limitations is effective for a period of four years from the commencement of the running of the statute. *California First Bank v Braden* (1989) 216 CA3d 672, 264 CR 820.

1 California Civil Procedure Before Trial §11.26 (Cal CEB 1977) has been replaced by 2 California Civil Procedure Before Trial §32.35 (3d ed Cal CEB 1990).

[§3.69] Cross-Complaint

1 California Civil Procedure Before Trial §§12.5–12.9 (Cal CEB 1977) have been replaced by 2 California Civil Procedure Before Trial §§33.6–33.14 (3d ed Cal CEB 1990).

4

Attachment

PRACTICE CONSIDERATIONS

[§4.5] Chart: Procedural Guide to Attachment

2. Code of Civil Procedure §484.330 has been amended to provide that the defendant must be served with a notice of application and hearing and a copy of the application at least 15 days before the hearing.

[§4.6] Checklist: Client Interview and Attachment Procedure

I. PRELIMINARY CONSIDERATIONS

A. Ascertain the facts

Two additional preliminary considerations are:

10. Is the debt unsecured or has the value of the collateral decreased through no fault of the creditor?

11. Does the debtor have a judgment against the creditor or has the debtor asserted a defense in its answer or filed a cross-complaint stating claims on which an attachment could be issued?

B. Evaluate the alternatives

3. 1, 2 California Civil Procedure Before Trial (2d ed Cal CEB 1977, 1978) have been replaced by 1, 2, 3 California Civil Procedure Before Trial (3d ed Cal CEB 1990). Note, however, that the new edition does not cover claim and delivery and attachment in depth.

II. PREPARATION FOR ATTACHMENT

Give required notice

1. Former Los Angeles Super Ct R 490B has been eliminated. The

required notice before an ex parte hearing is now covered by Los Angeles Super Ct R 9.37, which requires notice by noon on the court day before the ex parte application will be made unless a shorter period is permitted on a showing that the required notification could not be given and that the moving party gave as much notification as possible. Similarly, San Francisco Super Ct R 3.5 provides that 24 hours' advance notice will be deemed reasonable notice under Cal Rules of Ct 379.

2. Code of Civil Procedure §484.040 no longer specifies that papers be served on the defendant at least 20 days before the hearing. Instead, the statute provides that service is governed by CCP §1005(b), which governs service of motions generally. For further discussion, see Update §4.24.

V. POSTHEARING PROCEDURES

E. Once the court issues a right to attach order, the plaintiff may utilize the procedures under the Civil Discovery Act (CCP §§2016–2036) to discover the identity, location, and value of property in which the defendant has an interest. CCP §485.230. Counsel should be aware that CCP §485.230 incorporates both the procedures and the protections of the Civil Discovery Act. See, *e.g.,* CCP §2023 regarding sanctions for misuse of the discovery process. For a comprehensive discussion of discovery, see Civil Discovery Practice in California (Cal CEB 1988).

2A California Forms of Pleading and Practice (1986) has been replaced by 2A California Forms of Pleading and Practice. Oakland: Matthew Bender & Co. (1992).

California State Sheriffs' Association Civil Procedure Manual (3d ed rev 1978) has been replaced by California State Sheriffs' Association Civil Procedure Manual (4th ed rev 1994).

[§4.7] Attachment as Debt Collection Remedy

On the availability of discovery procedures to investigate an attachment debtor's assets after issuance of a right to attach order, see CCP §485.230, discussed in Update §4.6.

Availability of Attachment

When Attachment Authorized

[§4.8] General Requirements

The injunction procedure may not be used as a method of circumventing attachment requirements. *Doyka v Superior Court* (1991) 233 CA3d 1134, 285 CR 14. In *Doyka,* the court of appeal overturned an injunction preventing the use of funds held in any of the defendant's bank accounts to secure repayment of a loan in that amount. Although the loan was partly secured by real property, the injunction failed to satisfy the requirements of CCP §483.010(b), which governs attachments concerning obligations secured by real property (see Book §4.11). The injunction also failed to comply with CCP §487.020(b), which exempts from attachment property necessary for the support of the defendant and the defendant's family (see Book §4.18).

[§4.10] Amount in Controversy

Former CCP §§116–117.9 have been repealed. On small claims court actions, now see CCP §§116.110–116.950, discussed in Update §2.24.

[§4.12] Commercial Transaction

The attachment of property belonging to a testamentary trust was allowed under CCP §483.010(c) in *Kadison, Pfaelzer, Woodard, Quinn & Rossi v Wilson* (1987) 197 CA3d 1, 242 CR 595. The court ruled that a trust is not a "natural person" within the meaning of the statute and that, even if the trust were a natural person, the underlying claim in *Kadison* arose out of the conduct of a "trade, business, or profession," which encompasses almost any activity engaged in for profit with frequency and continuity. Section 483.010(c) is intended to limit attachments to commercial transactions and to preclude them in consumer transactions.

Whose Property Can Be Attached

Resident Debtors

[§4.14] Natural Person

The term "person" now includes a natural person, a corporation, a partnership or other unincorporated association, a limited liability company, and a public entity. CCP §481.170.

WRITS OF ATTACHMENT

Procedure on Noticed Hearing

[§4.20] Applying for Attachment

Although CCP §484.020(e) requires the attachment application to describe the defendant's property with specificity, it does not prohibit a plaintiff from targeting for attachment everything a defendant owns, as long as the property descriptions permit the defendant to identify the property sought to be attached. *Bank of America v Salinas Nissan, Inc.* (1989) 207 CA3d 260, 268, 254 CR 748, 753.

For further discussion of necessary averments in the plaintiff's affidavit, see Update §4.34.

[§4.22] Undertakings To Obtain Writ of Attachment or Temporary Protective Order

For an attachment to be valid, the plaintiff *must* file an undertaking *before* issuance of the attachment. *Vershbow v Reiner* (1991) 231 CA3d 879, 282 CR 684. Emphasizing that attachment statutes are strictly construed, the court in *Vershbow* rejected the argument that an attachment, despite the lack of an undertaking, is still valid if the writ of attachment is recorded, the defendant fails to object to its sufficiency, or the court clerk mistakenly issues the writ.

Notice of Hearing

[§4.24] Serving Notice on Defendant

Code of Civil Procedure §484.040 no longer specifies that moving papers must be served on the defendant at least 20 days before the hearing. Instead, the statute provides that service is governed by CCP §1005(b), which sets time limits for the service of motions generally. See also CCP §1005(a)(1). Under CCP §1005(b), all moving and supporting papers must be served and filed at least 15 calendar days before the time scheduled for hearing, unless otherwise ordered or specifically provided by law. When notice is served by mail, the period is increased by 5 days if the place of mailing and the place of address is within the state of California. There is a 10-day increase if the place of mailing or the address is outside the state but within the United States. There is a 20-day increase if either the place of mailing or address is outside the United States.

An additional writ of attachment may be obtained if the plaintiff serves the defendant a notice of application and hearing and a copy of the application at least 15 days before the hearing. CCP §484.330.

Opposing Issuance of Writ of Attachment

[§4.26] Notice of Opposition

Papers filed in opposition to a noticed application for a right to attach order or writ of attachment are now subject to CCP §1005(b). See CCP §§484.040, 1005. Under CCP §1005(b), all papers opposing a motion noticed under CCP §1005(b) must be filed with the court and served on each party at least five court days before the time appointed for the hearing. Reply papers must be served and filed at least two court days before the date scheduled for the hearing.

On the plaintiff's right to file a reply memorandum, see Update §4.26A.

Counsel opposing an application for a writ of attachment should determine whether the proper undertaking has been filed by the plaintiff. A writ of attachment issued by the clerk without the mandatory undertaking is void *ab initio*. *Vershbow v Reiner* (1991) 231 CA3d 879, 282 CR 684.

The Los Angeles Law Departments Policy Manual referred to in the Book has been eliminated. Now see the Los Angeles Superior Court Rules.

[§4.26A] Plaintiff's Reply

A plaintiff seeking the issuance of a "right to attach order" may now file and serve on the opposing party a reply memorandum two court days before the hearing date. CCP §484.060(c).

Claim of Exemption

[§§4.28, 4.32] Procedure; Opposing Claim of Exemption

A defendant need not prove that property is exempt unless the plaintiff serves and files a timely notice of opposition to the claim of exemption. *Bank of America v Salinas Nissan, Inc.* (1989) 207 CA3d 260, 270, 254 CR 748, 755.

Noticed Hearing

Findings and Determinations

[§4.34] Requirements of Court

A party seeking a writ of attachment on an originally secured claim has the burden of proving that the security has diminished in value and that the party was not responsible for that diminution. CCP §483.010(b). However, it is not necessary for the moving party's affidavit to contain such averments. *Bank of America v Salinas Nissan, Inc.* (1989) 207 CA3d 260, 273, 254 CR 748. The court in *Salinas Nissan* also held that the trial court need not make a *specific* finding regarding responsibility for any diminution in the security's value. Such a finding was implicit when the declarations had sufficiently dealt with the issue.

[§4.37A] Right To Renew Application for Attachment

The trial court may entertain and grant a second application for a right to attach order. *Film Packages, Inc. v Brandywine Film Prods., Ltd.* (1987) 193 CA3d 824, 238 CR 623. In *Brandywine,* the court upheld the use of newly obtained deposition testimony as the basis for a second application. Although no new facts were revealed in the depositions, the testimony produced "new evidence of the meaning of those facts." 193 CA3d at 829. Moreover, the court held that trial courts have inherent power to reconsider previous motions "based on a fuller statement of facts previously furnished," notwithstanding limitations in CCP §1008(b). 193 CA3d at 830. (Code of Civil Procedure §§1008(b) and 484.100 provide statutory authority for later motions.)

Since *Brandywine,* CCP §1008(b) has been amended to provide that such applications may be made based on "new or different facts, circumstances, or law." Counsel should bear in mind, however, that CCP §1008(a) and (e) now require a party making the application to declare, in addition to the new information, what order or decisions were previously made.

Counsel should be alert to evidence uncovered in discovery which might persuade a trial judge to grant the order on a second application.

Levy Procedure

[§4.39] Practice Considerations

On the availability of discovery procedures to investigate a defendant's assets after issuance of a right to attach order, see CCP §485.230, discussed in Update §4.6.

[§4.43] Instructions to Levying Officer

California State Sheriffs' Association Civil Procedure Manual (3d ed rev 1978) has been replaced by California State Sheriffs' Association Civil Procedural Manual (4th ed rev 1994).

Levy

Levying Officer

[§4.45] Statutory Authority

Effective January 1, 1997, the definition of levying officer no longer includes constables. Only sheriffs or marshals are levying officers. CCP §481.140.

[§4.46] Levying Officer's Duties Before Levy

Former Code of Civil Procedure §1032.8 was repealed in 1986 and replaced by CCP §1033.5(a)(4), which allows the fees of a registered process server to be recovered as costs.

Lien of Attachment

[§4.53] Effect of Lien

See *Louis & Diederich, Inc. v Cambridge European Imports, Inc.* (1987) 189 CA3d 1574, 234 CR 889, which illustrates the value of perfecting a security interest in attached property to avoid losing the property to later purchasers. On the perfection of security interests in general, see Secured Transactions in California Commercial Law Practice, chap 3 (Cal CEB 1986); see also Taking Security Interests in Personal Property (Cal CEB Action Guide Spring 1993) and Enforcing Security Interests in Personal Property (Cal CEB Action Guide Fall 1994).

[§4.59] Management and Disposition of Attached Property

Former Cal Rules of Ct 238–240, governing the ex parte appointment and confirmation of a receiver, have been repealed and replaced by Cal Rules of Ct 349–353. The rules governing appointment of receivers in Los Angeles Superior Court are now set forth in Los Angeles Super Ct R 9.51.

EX PARTE WRITS OF ATTACHMENT

[§4.67] Applying for Ex Parte Writ

Code of Civil Procedure §485.010 has been amended to allow the defendant's "insolvency" to support a finding of great or irreparable injury. To establish the threat of injury under this standard, the plaintiff must show facts permitting the court to infer under the circumstances that the defendant has failed to pay the debt underlying the requested attachment and that the defendant is insolvent, *i.e.,* his or her debts are not being paid as they become due, unless they are subject to a bona fide dispute. In addition to the requirements of CCP §485.010, the plaintiff's affidavit supporting the ex parte attachment must state the defendant's known undisputed debts, the fact that the debts are not subject to bona fide dispute, and the basis for the plaintiff's determination that the defendant's debts are undisputed. CCP §485.010(b)(2).

Former CCP §§485.010(b)(2), 485.010(b)(3), 485.010(b)(4) have been renumbered CCP §§485.010(b)(3), 485.010(b)(4), and 485.010(b)(5), respectively.

Debtor's Remedies

[§4.71] Quashing Ex Parte Writ of Attachment

After an ex parte writ of attachment is issued under CCP §485.010(b)(2) (great or irreparable injury established based on a showing of the defendant's insolvency), the defendant may request the court to review the issuance of the writ. The court must conduct a hearing within five court days after the plaintiff is served with notice of the defendant's request. CCP §485.010(c).

TEMPORARY PROTECTIVE ORDERS

Obtaining Temporary Protective Order

[§4.83] Procedure

The Los Angeles Law Department Policy Manual has been replaced by the Los Angeles Superior Court Rules.

Modification, Vacation, or Termination of Temporary Protective Order

[§4.89] Procedure

The references to CCP §489.410 in Book §4.89 should be to CCP §489.320.

INSOLVENT DEFENDANT

[§4.100] General Assignment for Benefit of Creditors

The reference to 11 USC §522.547 in Book §4.100 should be to 11 USC §547; see also 11 USC §551.

[§4.103] Subrogation of Assignee

The last paragraph in Book §4.103 should read: "On the filing of a petition commencing a case under Title 11 of the United States Code, a lien terminated under CCP §§493.010–493.060 is preserved for the benefit of the estate. CCP §493.060(b)."

5

Claim and Delivery

MISCELLANEOUS PREJUDGMENT CREDITORS' REMEDIES

[§5.38] Real Property

California Real Property Sales Transactions §§12.86–12.92 (Cal CEB 1981), cited in Book §5.38, have been superseded by California Lis Pendens Practice (2d ed Cal CEB 1994).

[§5.39] Mechanics' Lien and Stop Notice

California Mechanics' Liens and Other Remedies (Cal CEB 1972) has been replaced by California Mechanics' Liens and Other Remedies (2d ed Cal CEB 1988).

[§5.41] Receivership

1 California Civil Procedure Before Trial, chap 18 (Cal CEB 1977) has been replaced by 2 California Civil Procedure Before Trial, chap 40 (3d ed Cal CEB 1990).

In an action by a secured lender for specified performance of an assignment of rents in a mortgage or deed of trust, appointment of a receiver is authorized by CCP §564(b)(10). Appointment is also authorized in a case brought by an assignee under an assignment of leases, rents, issues, or profits under to CC §2938(g). CCP §564(b)(11).

6

Obtaining, Renewal, and Satisfaction of Judgment

[§6.1] SCOPE

1, 2 California Civil Procedure Before Trial (2d ed Cal CEB 1977, 1978) have been replaced by 1, 2, 3 California Civil Procedure Before Trial (3d ed Cal CEB 1990).

1, 2 California Civil Procedure During Trial (Cal CEB 1982, 1984) have been replaced by 1, 2, 3 California Trial Practice: Civil Procedure During Trial (3d ed Cal CEB 1995).

DISCOVERY

[§6.2] In General; Statutory Authority

Effective July 1, 1987, CCP §§2016–2036 (the Civil Discovery Act of 1986) repealed and replaced former CCP §§2016–2037.9.

Former Cal Rules of Ct 333 has been repealed. For time limitations on discovery preceding trial, now see CCP §2024, which is substantially similar to former Cal Rules of Ct 333.

Rules governing economic litigation for municipal and justice courts (CCP §§90–100) still affect permissible discovery in many cases. For a comprehensive discussion of the new discovery statutes, see 1, 2 Civil Discovery Practice in California (Cal CEB 1988).

1 California Civil Procedure During Trial, chap 10 (Cal CEB 1982) has been replaced by 2 California Trial Practice: Civil Procedure During Trial, chap 12 (3d ed Cal CEB 1995).

[§6.3] Particular Applicability of Requests for Admissions

For a thorough discussion of requests for admissions, including appropriate forms, see 2 Civil Discovery Practice in California, chap 11 (Cal CEB 1988).

1 California Civil Procedure During Trial §§10.61–10.62 (Cal CEB 1982) have been replaced by 2 California Trial Practice: Civil Procedure During Trial, §§12.122–12.134 (3d ed Cal CEB 1995).

DEFAULT JUDGMENTS

[§6.5] Procedural Guide

On page 397 in Book §6.5, under the heading "Issuance and Recording of Abstract of Judgment," the citation for notice of judgment lien should be CCP §697.510. The following citation should appear at the end of the last line on page 397: Cal Rules of Ct 2–3, 122–123. The same citation should appear on page 399 after "Last day to file appeal" (under the heading "Expiration Date for Appeal or Other Relief") and after the last line on page 401. The citation to CCP §586(b) on page 398 should be to CCP §586(6).

[§6.6] Entry of Default

Effective January 1, 1994, CCP §585(c) was amended to require entry of default before the rendering of a default judgment when service has been made by publication.

[§6.7] Judicial Council Form 982(a)(6): Request for Entry of Default

ATTORNEY OR PARTY WITHOUT ATTORNEY *(Name and Address)*: TELEPHONE NO.: FOR COURT USE ONLY

ATTORNEY FOR *(Name)*:

Insert name of court and name of judicial district and branch court, if any:

PLAINTIFF:

DEFENDANT:

REQUEST FOR (Application) ☐ **ENTRY OF DEFAULT** ☐ **CLERK'S JUDGMENT** ☐ **COURT JUDGMENT**

CASE NUMBER:

1. TO THE CLERK: On the complaint or cross-complaint filed
   a. On *(date)*:
   b. By *(name)*:
   c. ☐ Enter default of defendant *(names)*:

   d. ☐ I request a court judgment under CCP 585(b), (c), 989, etc. *(Testimony required. Apply to the clerk for a hearing date, unless the court will enter a judgment on an affidavit under CCP 585(d).)*
   e. ☐ Enter clerk's judgment
      (1) ☐ For restitution of the premises only and issue a writ of execution on the judgment. CCP 1174(c) does not apply. (CCP 1169) ☐ Include in the judgment all tenants, subtenants, named claimants, and other occupants of the premises. The Prejudgment Claim of Right to Possession was served in compliance with CCP 415.46.
      (2) ☐ Under CCP 585(a). *(Complete the declaration under CCP 585.5 on the reverse (item 4).)*
      (3) ☐ For default previously entered on *(date)*:

2. **Judgment to be entered**

	Amount	Credits Acknowledged	Balance
a. Demand of complaint	$	$	$
b. Statement of damages (CCP 425.11) *(superior court only)*†			
(1) Special	$	$	$
(2) General	$	$	$
c. Interest	$	$	$
d. Costs *(see reverse)*	$	$	$
e. Attorney fees	$	$	$
f. **TOTALS**	$	$	$

   g. **Daily damages** were demanded in complaint at the rate of: $ per day beginning *(date)*:

3. ☐ *(check if filed in an unlawful detainer case)* **UNLAWFUL DETAINER ASSISTANT** information is on the reverse *(complete item 3)*.

Date:

(TYPE OR PRINT NAME) ▶ (SIGNATURE OF PLAINTIFF OR ATTORNEY FOR PLAINTIFF)

† *Personal injury or wrongful death actions only.*

FOR COURT USE ONLY
(1) ☐ Default entered as requested on *(date)*:
(2) ☐ Default NOT entered as requested *(state reason)*:

Clerk, by: ______________

(Continued on reverse)

Form Adopted by the Judicial Council of California 982(a)(6) [Rev. July 1, 1996*]

REQUEST FOR ENTRY OF DEFAULT (Application to Enter Default)

Code of Civil Procedure, §§ 585-587, 1169

*See note on reverse

SHORT TITLE:	CASE NUMBER:

3. **UNLAWFUL DETAINER ASSISTANT** *(Business and Professions Code sections 6400–6415)* An **unlawful detainer assistant**
☐ did **not** ☐ did for compensation give advice or assistance with this form. *(If declarant has received **any** help or advice for pay from an unlawful detainer assistant, state)*:
a. Assistant's name: b. Telephone No.:
c. Street address, city, and ZIP:

d. County of registration: e. Registration No.: f. Expires on *(date)*

4. ☐ **DECLARATION UNDER CCP 585.5** *(Required for clerk's judgment under CCP 585(a))* This action
a. ☐ is ☐ is not on a contract or installment sale for goods or services subject to CC 1801, etc. (Unruh Act).
b. ☐ is ☐ is not on a conditional sales contract subject to CC 2981, etc. (Rees-Levering Motor Vehicle Sales and Finance Act).
c. ☐ is ☐ is not on an obligation for goods, services, loans, or extensions of credit subject to CCP 395(b).

5. **DECLARATION OF MAILING (CCP 587)** A copy of this Request for Entry of Default was
a. ☐ **not mailed** to the following defendants whose addresses are **unknown** to plaintiff or plaintiff's attorney *(names)*:

b. ☐ **mailed** first-class, postage prepaid, in a sealed envelope addressed to each defendant's attorney of record or, if none, to each defendant's last known address as follows:
(1) Mailed on *(date)*: (2) To *(specify names and addresses shown on the envelopes)*:

I declare under penalty of perjury under the laws of the State of California that the foregoing items 3, 4, and 5 are true and correct.
Date:

.... ▶ ______________________________
(TYPE OR PRINT NAME) (SIGNATURE OF DECLARANT)

6. **MEMORANDUM OF COSTS** *(Required if judgment requested)* **Costs and Disbursements** are as follows (CCP 1033.5):
a. Clerk's filing fees .... $
b. Process server's fees .... $
c. Other *(specify)*: .... $
d. .... $
e. **TOTAL** .... $ ______________
f. ☐ Costs and disbursements are waived.

I am the attorney, agent, or party who claims these costs. To the best of my knowledge and belief this memorandum of costs is correct and these costs were necessarily incurred in this case.

I declare under penalty of perjury under the laws of the State of California that the foregoing is true and correct.
Date:

.... ▶ ______________________________
(TYPE OR PRINT NAME) (SIGNATURE OF DECLARANT)

7. ☐ **DECLARATION OF NONMILITARY STATUS** *(Required for a judgment)* No defendant named in item 1c of the application is in the military service so as to be entitled to the benefits of the Soldiers' and Sailors' Civil Relief Act of 1940 (50 U.S.C. appen. § 501 et seq.).

I declare under penalty of perjury under the laws of the State of California that the foregoing is true and correct.
Date:

.... ▶ ______________________________
(TYPE OR PRINT NAME) (SIGNATURE OF DECLARANT)

**NOTE:* Continued use of form 982(a)(6) (Rev. Sept. 30, 1991) is authorized until June 30, 1997, *except* in unlawful detainer proceedings.

Default Judgment

[§6.9] In General; Procedure

In order to obtain an enforceable default judgment against a corporation, the plaintiff must name and serve the corporation in its corporate capacity. *Earl W. Schott, Inc. v Kalar* (1993) 20 CA4th 943, 24 CR2d 580. The court in *Schott* ruled that the default judgment obtained by the plaintiff was ineffective against Kalar Construction Co., Inc., because the complaint named only Gary Kalar, individually and doing business as Kalar Construction. The plaintiff never named the corporation in its complaint nor served an individual as a representative of the corporation.

2 California Civil Procedure Before Trial §§30.35–30.80 (Cal CEB 1978) has been replaced by 3 California Civil Procedure Before Trial §§56.34–56.72 (3d ed Cal CEB 1990).

[§6.10] Form: Default Judgment by Clerk

Former Los Angeles Super Ct R 402 has been renumbered Los Angeles Super Ct R 3.2.

Relief From Default

[§6.12] In General

Motions to set aside a default or default judgment and for leave to defend actions under CCP §473.5, and motions to set aside default and for leave to amend under CCP §585.5, now require written notice to be given to all parties, as prescribed by CCP §1005(b). CCP §1005(a)(10), (12).

Shamblin v Brattain (1988) 44 C3d 474, 243 CR 902, illustrates the importance of *promptly* moving to obtain relief from default. See also *County of Stanislaus v Johnson* (1996) 43 CA4th 832, 51 CR2d 73; *Lorenz v Commercial Acceptance Ins. Co.* (1995) 40 CA4th 981, 47 CR2d 362; *Taylor v Varga* (1995) 37 CA4th 750, 43 CR2d 904; *Bonzer v City of Huntington Park* (1993) 20 CA4th 1474, 25 CR2d 278. Code of Civil Procedure §473 makes attorneys accountable for their own conduct when attorney conduct forms a basis for the motion. Whenever relief from default is granted based on an attorney's affidavit of fault, the court *must* direct the attorney to pay reasonable compensatory legal fees and costs to opposing counsel or parties. Moreover, whenever relief from a default judgment is granted under CCP §473, the court in its discretion may (1) impose a penalty of no more than $1000 on an offending attorney or defaulting party, (2) direct an offending attorney to pay an amount of no more than $1000 to the State Bar Client Security Fund, or (3) grant such other relief as is appropriate. Note that a penalty, when justified, may be assessed directly against the party as well as the attorney.

[§6.13] Small Claims Actions

Former CCP §117.8 has been repealed and replaced by CCP §§116.720–116.740.

A defendant who fails to appear at a small claims hearing has no right to appeal but may file a motion to vacate the judgment under CCP §116.730 (motion to vacate for lack of appearance) or CCP §116.740 (motion to vacate for improper service) and may appeal the denial of that motion. The motion must be filed in small claims court within 30 days after the notice of entry of judgment has been mailed. CCP §116.730(a). If the motion is granted and all the parties are present at the hearing on the motion and agree, the court may hear the case without rescheduling it. If the plaintiff is not present, the judge or clerk must reschedule the case and give notice under CCP §116.330. CCP §116.730(d). If the court denies the motion, the defendant may appeal to the superior court only on the denial of the motion to vacate. CCP §116.730(e). If the superior court decides that defendant's motion to vacate the judgment should have been granted, the court may hear the claims of all parties without rescheduling the matter, provided that all parties are present and the defendant has previously complied with these rules, or the court may order the case transferred to the small claims court for a hearing. CCP §116.730(f).

A plaintiff who fails to appear at the hearing in small claims court may move to vacate a default judgment entered for failure to appear. CCP §116.720. The motion must be filed within 30 days after the notice of entry of judgment is mailed. CCP §116.720(a). The earliest the clerk may schedule the hearing is 10 days after written notice has been mailed by the clerk to the parties. CCP §116.720(b). The motion may be granted on a showing of "good cause." If the defendant is absent from the hearing on the motion, the motion may be heard without the defendant. CCP §116.720(c). If the motion is granted and all parties are present and consent, the court may hear the case without recalendaring. If the motion to vacate the default judgment is granted in the defendant's absence, the matter will be reset and noticed under CCP §116.330. CCP §116.720(d).

OTHER JUDGMENTS WITHOUT TRIAL

Judgment by Consent or Stipulation

[§6.14] In General

Recoverable attorney fees are generally an item of costs under CC §1717(a). When the stipulation for judgment is silent on the matter of attorney fees but the contract in question provides for their recovery, the "party prevailing on the contract" will be entitled to recover attorney fees. *Lanyi v Goldblum* (1986) 177 CA3d 181, 223 CR 32. To avoid disputes, it is important to cover attorney fees in the stipulation for judgment. *Lanyi* actually concerned a settlement under CCP §998; however, the court's reasoning was based on general contract principles and should apply to other settlements as well. See also *Crib Retaining Walls, Inc. v NBS/Lowry, Inc.* (1996) 47 CA4th 886, 54 CR2d 850, commenting on *Rappenecker v Sea-Land Serv., Inc.* (1979) 93 CA3d 256, 155 CR 516, cited in Book §6.14.

2 California Civil Procedure Before Trial, chap 34 (Cal CEB 1978) has been replaced by 3 California Civil Procedure Before Trial, chap 60 (3d ed Cal CEB 1990).

[§6.15] Local Rules

The Los Angeles Law Departments Policy Manual has been replaced by the Los Angeles Superior Court Rules. Ex parte rules are now covered in Los Angeles Super Ct R 9.36–9.41.

[§6.16] Form: Stipulation for Judgment

Stipulations for judgment should indicate clearly whether the judgment is to include costs and, if so, whether costs include attorney fees. Specific amounts for fees and costs should also be listed.

[§§6.17–6.18] Forms: Judgment Pursuant to Stipulation by Debtor; Judgment by Default (Against One Defendant) and by Stipulation (of Another Defendant)

The judgment forms in Book §§6.17 and 6.18 both specify fees and costs. Liability for fees and costs, however, depends on the terms of the stipulation and possibly on the terms of the contract on which the eventual settlement was based.

Former Los Angeles Super Ct R 401, §2 has been renumbered Los Angeles Super Ct R 3.0(b).

Acceptance of Offer To Compromise Under CCP §998

[§6.19] Time Limitations

The effect of an offer that was made but not accepted, when the nonoffering party fails to obtain a more favorable judgment, is now governed by CCP §998(c)–(e).

2 California Civil Procedure Before Trial §§33.10–33.15 (Cal CEB 1978) have been replaced by 3 California Civil Procedure Before Trial, chap 67 (3d ed Cal CEB 1990). 1 California Civil Procedure During Trial §§3.30–3.33 have been replaced by 3 California Trial Practice: Civil Procedure During Trial §§27.51–27.58 (3d ed Cal CEB 1995).

[§6.20] Form: Offer To Compromise Under CCP §998

2 California Civil Procedure Before Trial §33.13 (Cal CEB 1978) has been replaced by 3 California Civil Procedure Before Trial §67.16 (3d ed Cal CEB 1990).

[§6.21] Form: Notice of Acceptance of Offer To Compromise

2 California Civil Procedure Before Trial §33.13 (Cal CEB 1978) has been replaced by 3 California Civil Procedure Before Trial §67.16 (3d ed Cal CEB 1990).

[§6.22] Confession of Judgment

On federal limitations on the use of confessions of judgment, see 16 CFR §444.2, discussed in Update §1.42. See also Update §2.21.

In *Rivercourt Co. v Dyna-Tel, Inc.* (1996) 41 CA4th 1477, 49 CR2d 279, the court affirmed the trial court's order setting aside a confession of judgment pursuant to CCP §473 on the ground that the judgment had been fraudulently entered.

[§6.23] Dismissal

2 California Civil Procedure Before Trial §§31.1–31.64 (Cal CEB 1978) have been replaced by 3 California Civil Procedure Before Trial, chap 57 (3d ed Cal CEB 1990). 2 California Civil Procedure Before Trial §§31.65–31.91 (Cal CEB 1978) have been replaced by 3 California Civil Procedure Before Trial, chap 58 (3d ed Cal CEB 1990).

The correct citation for *MacDonald v Joslyn*, cited in Book §6.23, is *MacDonald v Joslyn* (1969) 275 CA2d 282, 79 CR 707.

The holding in *International Indus., Inc. v Olen,* discussed in Book §6.23, has been largely superseded by subsequent legislative developments, including the enactment of CCP §§1032 and 1033.5. For an extensive discussion and criticism of *Olen,* see *Kelley v Bredelis* (1996) 45 CA4th 1819, 53 CR2d 536. See also *Hosking v Carrier Corp.* (review granted Mar. 26, 1997, S058301; superseded opinion at 50 CA4th 1641 (advance reports), 58 CR2d 617), and *Ryder v Peterson* (1996) 51 CA4th 1056, 59 CR2d 562, reaching opposite results regarding whether a party to a contract containing an attorney fees clause can recover fees after voluntary dismissal of the action on the contract.

[§6.24] Judgment on the Pleadings

1 California Civil Procedure Before Trial, chap 13 (Cal CEB 1977) has been replaced by 2 California Civil Procedure Before Trial, chap 34 (3d ed Cal CEB 1990). 1 California Civil Procedure During Trial §§6.43–6.45 have been replaced by 1 California Trial Practice: Civil Procedure During Trial §§6.94–6.96 (3d ed Cal CEB 1995).

Summary Judgment

[§6.25] In General

Code of Civil Procedure §437c now provides that if the notice of motion is served by facsimile transmission, express mail, or another method of overnight delivery, the required 28-day period of notice is increased by two court days.

Any objections to affidavits or declarations submitted in support of or in opposition to a motion for summary judgment on the ground that they (1) are not made on personal knowledge, (2) do not set forth admissible evidence, or (3) fail to affirmatively show that the affiant is competent to testify to the matters stated in the affidavits or declarations are waived unless made at or before the hearing. CCP §437c(d).

Code of Civil Procedure §437c(f) provides that a party may move for summary adjudication of a cause of action, an affirmative defense, a claim for damages, or an issue of duty. Effective January 1, 1994, CCP §437c(f) was amended to state that summary adjudication may only be granted "if it completely disposes of a cause of action, an affirmative defense, a claim for damages, or an issue of duty."

2 California Civil Procedure Before Trial, chap 29 (Cal CEB 1978) has been replaced by 2 California Civil Procedure Before Trial, chaps 43–47 (3d ed Cal CEB 1990).

[§6.26] Sample Form: Declaration in Support of Motion for Summary Judgment (Book Account)

2 California Civil Procedure Before Trial §29.75 (Cal CEB 1978) has been replaced by 2 California Civil Procedure Before Trial §46.26 (3d ed Cal CEB 1990).

[§6.27] Sample Form: Declaration by Assignee in Support of Motion for Summary Judgment (Book Account)

2 California Civil Procedure Before Trial §§29.75, 29.78 (Cal CEB 1978) have been replaced by 2 California Civil Procedure Before Trial §§46.26–46.27 (3d ed Cal CEB 1990).

JUDGMENT AFTER TRIAL

[§6.28] Trial by Court or Jury

2 California Civil Procedure Before Trial §§26.28–26.37 (Cal CEB 1978) have been replaced by 2 California Civil Procedure Before Trial, chap 50 (3d ed Cal CEB 1990). 1 California Civil Procedure During Trial §§7.1–7.17 have been replaced by 1 California Trial Practice: Civil Procedure During Trial §§8.1–8.18 (3d ed Cal CEB 1995).

[§6.29] Statement of Decision

A request for a statement of decision must now be made before submission of the matter for decision if the trial lasts less than one calendar day or less than eight hours in total. CCP §632.

2 California Civil Procedure During Trial §§20.16–20.26 (Cal CEB 1984) have been replaced by 3 California Trial Practice: Civil Procedure During Trial §§24.34–24.52 (3d ed Cal CEB 1995).

Drafting Judgment

[§6.30] In General

On the equitable power of a court to amend a judgment to add a judgment debtor on the theory that an entity is the alter ego of the original judgment debtor, see *Hall, Goodhue, Haisley & Barker, Inc. v Marconi Conference Ctr. Bd.* (1996) 41 CA4th 1551, 49 CR2d 286. As a general rule, a court may amend its judgment at any time so that the judgment will properly designate the real defendants. See also *Milrot v Stamper Med. Corp.* (1996) 44 CA4th 182, 51 CR2d 424; *Carr v Barnabey's Hotel Corp.* (1994) 23 CA4th 14, 28 CR2d 127; *NEC Elec. Inc. v Hurt* (1989) 208 CA3d 772, 256 CR 441; *Dow Jones Co. v Avenel* (1984) 151 CA3d 144, 198 CR 457.

2 California Civil Procedure During Trial §§21.9–21.14 (Cal CEB 1984) have been replaced by 3 California Trial Practice: Civil Procedure During Trial §§23.13–23.18 (3d ed Cal CEB 1995).

Costs

[§6.34] Statutory Authority

2 California Civil Procedure During Trial §§22.2–22.65 (Cal CEB 1984) have been replaced by 3 California Trial Practice: Civil Procedure During Trial §§27.3–27.111 (3d ed Cal CEB 1995).

Selected Cost Provisions

[§6.35] Effect of CCP §998 Offer

Code of Civil Procedure §998(e) provides that if the plaintiff fails to obtain a judgment more favorable than the defendant's offer to compromise, defendant's costs are to be deducted from any damages awarded to plaintiff. If the costs exceed the damages awarded to plaintiff, the net amount is awarded to the defendant and a judgment is entered accordingly. Effective January 1, 1995, CCP §998(c) provides that a plaintiff in a cause of action not based on tort shall not be deemed to have obtained a more favorable judgment unless the judgment, exclusive of attorney fees and costs, exceeds the offer made by defendant.

2 California Civil Procedure Before Trial §§33.10–33.15 (Cal CEB

1978) have been replaced by 3 California Civil Procedure Before Trial, chap 67 (3d ed Cal CEB 1990). 1 and 2 California Civil Procedure During Trial §§3.30–3.33, 22.20–22.22 (Cal CEB 1984) have been replaced by 3 California Trial Practice: Civil Procedure During Trial §§23.2, 27.51–27.66 (3d ed Cal CEB 1995).

[§6.40] Procedure

2 California Civil Procedure During Trial §§22.54–22.64 (Cal CEB 1984) have been replaced by 3 California Trial Practice: Civil Procedure During Trial §§27.88–27.111 (3d ed Cal CEB 1995).

[§6.41] Attorneys' Fees

Code of Civil Procedure §1033.5(a)(10)(A) provides that attorney fees authorized by *contract* may be recovered as an item of costs. The award of these fees is made on noticed motion or on entry of a default judgment, unless the parties stipulate otherwise. CCP §1033.5(c)(5).

Parties need no longer make a noticed motion to compel the court to determine the amount of reasonable attorney fees under CC §1717: "Reasonable attorney's fees shall be fixed by the court, and shall be an element of the costs of suit." CC §1717(a). See also CCP §1033.5(c)(5) (attorney fees awarded under CC §1717 are allowable as costs under CCP §1032).

A party may, however, by noticed motion, require the court to determine the "party prevailing on the contract" for the purpose of CC §1717. CC §1717(b)(1). The phrase "party prevailing on the contract" has been substituted for "prevailing party" throughout the statute. Moreover, except as provided in CC §1717(b)(2) (see discussion in Book §6.41), the "party prevailing on the contract" is the party who recovered a greater relief in the action *on the contract*. The court may also determine that no party has prevailed on the contract for purposes of the statute. These amendments make it clear that in suits that include other causes of action, the party prevailing on the contract cause of action is entitled to recover attorney fees based on a provision in that contract, even though damages may be awarded against that party on other causes of action.

Whether a particular action is "on the contract" under CC §1717(b)(1) depends on the allegations in the plaintiff's complaint. Even when a breach of contract is not specifically pleaded, however, the action may still be considered "on a contract" when the contract claim is asserted at trial and the contractual theory of recovery is known to the court and opposing counsel. *Walsh v New West Fed. Sav. & Loan Ass'n* (1991) 234 CA3d 1539, 1547, 1 CR2d 35, 40.

Civil Code §1717.5 provides that in any action on a contract based on a book account that does not provide for attorney fees and costs under CC §1717, the prevailing party on the contract is entitled to reasonable attorney fees in addition to other costs. This applies to contracts entered on or after January 1, 1987. Rights under CC §1717.5 may be waived by the parties and are limited by any contrary statutory provisions. Fees under CC §1717.5 are fixed by the court and are treated as part of the costs of suit. The fees cannot exceed the lesser of $660 or 25 percent of the principal obligation owing under the contract. If a party is found to have no obligation on a book account, the court must award that party reasonable attorney fees, not to exceed $660.

Civil Code §1717.5 does not apply if there is a written agreement between the parties signed by the person to be charged, unless that agreement states that the prevailing party in an action between the parties is entitled to the fees under the statute. Similarly, the statute does not apply to any action in which an insurance company is a party; nor is any insurance company, surety, or guarantor liable under the statute for attorney fees and costs awarded to a party prevailing against its insured, without a specific contractual provision authorizing such liability. Also, the statute does not apply to any action in which certain specified kinds of banking institutions are parties. CC §1717.5.

California Rules of Court 870.2, cited in Book §6.41, has been replaced by a new version of the rule, effective January 1, 1994. A notice of motion to claim attorney fees for services up to and including judgment must be served and filed within the time for filing a notice of appeal under Cal Rules of Ct 2 and 3. The parties may also extend the time for making the motion by filing a stipulation before the expiration of the above time period. The deadline may be extended up to 60 days after expiration of the time for filing notice of appeal or, if a notice of appeal is filed, until the time within which a memorandum of costs must be served and filed under Cal Rules of Ct 26(d). The trial judge may also extend the time for filing a motion for attorney fees on a showing of good cause. Cal Rules of Ct 870.2(b).

A notice of motion to claim attorney fees on appeal under a statute or contract requiring the court to determine entitlement to the fees, the amount of the fees, or both, must be served and filed within the time for serving and filing the memorandum of costs under Cal Rules of Ct 26(d). Cal Rules of Ct 870.2(c). If a party is entitled to statutory or contractual attorney fees that are fixed without the necessity of a court determination, the fees must be claimed in the memorandum of costs. Cal Rules of Ct 870.2(d).

The reference in Book §6.41 to Contra Costa Super Ct R 22(c) should now be to Contra Costa Super Ct R 22(d) and (f).

2 California Civil Procedure During Trial §§22.66–22.89 (Cal CEB 1984) have been replaced by 3 California Trial Practice: Civil Procedure During Trial, chap 26 (3d ed Cal CEB 1995).

[§6.42] Interest

2 California Civil Procedure During Trial §§22.90–22.95 (Cal CEB 1984) have been replaced by 3 California Trial Practice: Civil Procedure During Trial §§27.112–27.127 (3d ed Cal CEB 1995).

[§6.43] Vacating Judgments; Appeals

Perfecting an appeal by filing a notice of appeal generally stays proceedings in the trial court, including enforcement of the judgment. CCP §916(a); Cal Rules of Ct 1(a).

2 California Civil Procedure During Trial, chap 19 (Cal CEB 1984) has been replaced by 3 California Trial Practice: Civil Procedure During Trial, chap 25 (3d ed Cal CEB 1995). 2 California Civil Procedure Before Trial §§30.51–30.80 (2d ed Cal CEB 1978) have been replaced by 3 California Civil Procedure Before Trial §§56.51–56.72 (3d ed Cal CEB 1990).

California Civil Appellate Practice (2d ed Cal CEB 1985) has been replaced by California Civil Appellate Practice (3d ed Cal CEB 1996).

STEPS TO ENFORCE JUDGMENT

Entry of Judgment

[§6.44] In General

Code of Civil Procedure §664.5, cited in Book §6.44, actually provides that, for purposes of a contested action other than a small claims court action or an action in which a prevailing party is not represented by counsel, the party submitting the judgment must prepare and mail a copy of the notice of entry of judgment to all parties who have appeared and file the original notice of entry and proof of service. CCP §664.5(a). Code of Civil Procedure §664.5(b) provides that when a prevailing party is not represented by counsel, the clerk of the court mails the notice of entry and executes a certificate of mailing.

For a form for a notice of entry of judgment, see 3 California Trial Practice: Civil Procedure During Trial §23.40 (3d ed Cal CEB 1995).

There is a mandatory form for the notice of entry of judgment in small claims court, prescribed by the California Judicial Council. Generally, the clerk of the court will deliver or mail the notice of entry of judgment in small claims proceedings. See CCP §116.610. A copy of this form can be found in Update §6.44A.

In addition to the statutory references in Book §6.44, see Cal Rules of Ct 2(a) regarding the relationship between the notice of entry of judgment and the time within which a notice of appeal can be filed.

2 California Civil Procedure During Trial §§21.15–21.18 (Cal CEB 1984) have been replaced by 3 California Trial Practice: Civil Procedure During Trial §§23.19–23.28 (3d ed Cal CEB 1995).

[§6.44A] Judicial Council Form SC-130: Notice of Entry of Judgment (Small Claims)

Name and Address of Court:

SMALL CLAIMS CASE NO.:

NOTICE TO ALL PLAINTIFFS AND DEFENDANTS: **Your small claims case has been decided. If you lost the case, and the court ordered you to pay money, your wages, money, and property may be taken without further warning from the court. Read the back of this sheet for important information about your rights.**	***AVISO A TODOS LOS DEMANDANTES Y DEMANDADOS:*** ***Su caso ha sido resuelto por la corte para reclamos judiciales menores. Si la corte ha decidido en su contra y ha ordenado que usted pague dinero, le pueden quitar su salario, su dinero, y otras cosas de su propiedad, sin aviso adicional por parte de esta corte. Lea el reverso de este formulario para obtener información de importancia acerca de sus derechos.***

PLAINTIFF/DEMANDANTE *(Name, street address, and telephone number of each)*	DEFENDANT/DEMANDADO *(Name, street address, and telephone number of each)*
Telephone No.	Telephone No.
Telephone No.	Telephone No.:

☐ See attached sheet for additional plaintiffs and defendants.

NOTICE OF ENTRY OF JUDGMENT

Judgment was entered as checked below on *(date)*:

1. ☐ Defendant *(name, if more than one)*:
   shall pay plaintiff *(name, if more than one)*:
   $ principal and $ costs on plaintiff's claim.
2. ☐ Defendant does not owe plaintiff any money on plaintiff's claim.
3. ☐ Plaintiff *(name, if more than one)*:
   shall pay defendant *(name, if more than one)*:
   $ principal and $ costs on defendant's claim.
4. ☐ Plaintiff does not owe defendant any money on defendant's claim.
5. ☐ Possession of the following property is awarded to plaintiff *(describe property)*:
6. ☐ Payments are to be made at the rate of $ per , beginning on *(date)*: and on the day of each month thereafter until paid in full. If any payment is missed, the entire balance may become due immediately.
7. ☐ Dismissed in court ☐ with prejudice. ☐ without prejudice.
8. ☐ *Attorney-Client Fee Dispute (Attachment to Notice of Entry of Judgment) (form SC-132)* is attached.
9. ☐ Other *(specify)*:
10. ☐ This judgment results from a motor vehicle accident on a California highway and was caused by the judgment debtor's operation of a motor vehicle. If the judgment is not paid, the judgment creditor may apply to have the judgment debtor's driver's license suspended.
11. Enforcement of the judgment is automatically postponed for 30 days or, if an appeal is filed, until the appeal is decided.
12. ☐ This notice was personally delivered to *(insert name and date)*:
13. CLERK'S CERTIFICATE OF MAILING—I certify that I am not a party to this action. This *Notice of Entry of Judgment* was mailed first class, postage prepaid, in a sealed envelope to the parties at the addresses shown above. The mailing and this certification occurred at the place and on the date shown below.

   Place of mailing: , California

   Date of mailing:

Clerk, by ____________________, Deputy

— The county provides small claims advisor services free of charge. Read the information sheet on the reverse. —

Form Adopted by the Judicial Council of California SC-130 [Rev. January 1, 1997]

NOTICE OF ENTRY OF JUDGMENT
(Small Claims)

Cal. Rules of Court, rule 982.7

INFORMATION AFTER JUDGMENT	*INFORMACION DESPUES DEL FALLO DE LA CORTE*

Your small claims case has been decided. The **judgment** or decision of the court appears on the front of this sheet. The court may have ordered one party to pay money to the other party. The person (or business) who won the case and who can collect the money is called the **judgment creditor**. The person (or business) who lost the case and who owes the money is called the **judgment debtor**.
Enforcement of the judgment is **postponed** until the time for appeal ends or until the appeal is decided. This means that the judgment creditor cannot collect any money or take any action until this period is over. Generally, both parties may be represented by lawyers after judgment.

IF YOU LOST THE CASE . . .

1. If you lost the case on your own claim and the court did not award you any money, the court's decision on your claim is **FINAL**. You may not appeal your own claim.
2. If you lost the case and the court ordered you to pay money, your money and property may be taken to pay the claim unless you do one of the following things:
   a. **PAY THE JUDGMENT**
   The law requires you to pay the amount of the judgment. You may pay the judgment creditor directly, or pay the judgment to the court for an additional fee. You may also ask the court to order monthly payments you can afford. Ask the clerk for information about these procedures.
   b. **APPEAL**
   If you disagree with the court's decision, you may appeal the decision *on the other party's claim*. You may not appeal the decision on your own claim. However, if any party appeals, there will be a new trial on *all* the claims. If you appeared at the trial, you *must* begin your appeal by filing a form called a *Notice of Appeal* and pay the required fees within *30 days* after the date this *Notice of Entry of Judgment* was mailed or handed to you at the time of the small claims hearing. Your appeal will be in the superior court. You will have a **new trial** and you must present your evidence again. You may be represented by a lawyer.
   c. **VACATE OR CANCEL THE JUDGMENT**
   If you did not go to the trial, you may ask the court to vacate or cancel the judgment. To make this request, you must file a *Motion to Vacate the Judgment* and pay the required fee *within 30 days* after the date this *Notice of Entry of Judgment* was mailed. If your request is denied, you then have *10 days* from the date the notice of denial was mailed to file an appeal.
   The period to file the *Motion to Vacate the Judgment* is *180 days* if you were *not properly served* with the claim. The 180-day period begins on the date you found out or should have found out about the judgment against you.

IF YOU WON THE CASE . . .

1. If you were sued by the other party and you won the case, then the other party may not appeal the court's decision.
2. If you won the case and the court awarded you money, here are some steps you may take to collect your money or get possession of your property:
   a. **COLLECTING FEES**
   Sometimes fees are charged for filing court papers or for serving the judgment debtor. These extra costs can become part of your original judgment. To claim these fees, ask the clerk for a *Memorandum of Costs*.
   b. **VOLUNTARY PAYMENT**
   Ask the judgment debtor to pay the money. If your claim was for possession of property, ask the judgment debtor to return the property to you. **THE COURT WILL NOT COLLECT THE MONEY OR ENFORCE THE JUDGMENT FOR YOU.**
   c. **STATEMENT OF ASSETS**
   If the judgment debtor does not pay the money, the law requires the debtor to fill out a form called the *Judgment Debtor's Statement of Assets*. This form will tell you what property the judgment debtor has that may be available to pay your claim. If the judgment debtor willfully fails to send you the completed form, you may ask the court to give you your attorney's fees and expenses, and other appropriate relief, after proper notice, under Code of Civil Procedure section 708.170.
   d. **ORDER OF EXAMINATION**
   You may also make the debtor come to court to answer questions about income and property. To do this, ask the clerk for an *Order of Examination* and pay the required fee. There is a fee if a law officer serves the order on the judgment debtor. You may also obtain the judgment debtor's financial records. Ask the clerk for the *Subpena Duces Tecum* form.
   e. **WRIT OF EXECUTION**
   After you find out about the judgment debtor's property, you may ask the court for a *Writ of Execution* and pay the required fee. A writ of execution is a court paper that tells a law officer to take property of the judgment debtor to pay your claim. Here are some examples of the kinds of property the officer may be able to take: **wages, bank account, automobile, business property, or rental income**. For some kinds of property, you may need to file other forms. See the law officer for information.
   f. **ABSTRACT OF JUDGMENT**
   The judgment debtor may own land or a house or other buildings. You may want to put a lien on the property so that you will be paid if the property is sold. You can get a lien by filing an *Abstract of Judgment* with the county recorder in the county where the property is located. The recorder will charge a fee for the *Abstract of Judgment*.

NOTICE TO THE PARTY WHO WON: As soon as you have been paid in full, you *must* fill out the form below and mail it to the court *immediately* or you may be fined. If an *Abstract of Judgment* has been recorded, you must use another form; see the clerk for the proper form.

SMALL CLAIMS CASE NO.:

ACKNOWLEDGMENT OF SATISFACTION OF JUDGMENT

(Do not use this form if an Abstract of Judgment *has been recorded.)*

To the Clerk of the Court:

I am the ☐ judgment creditor. ☐ assignee of record.

I agree that the judgment in this action has been paid in full or otherwise satisfied.

Date:

(TYPE OR PRINT NAME) (SIGNATURE)

SC-130 [Rev. January 1, 1997] **NOTICE OF ENTRY OF JUDGMENT (Small Claims)** Page two

Comment: Generally, the clerk of the court will deliver or mail the notice of entry of judgment in small claims proceedings. See CCP §116.610.

[§6.45] Judgments Based on Sister-State Judgments

Recordation of a sister-state judgment will not, by itself, give rise to a judgment lien on real property located in California. The creditor first must reduce the sister-state judgment to a California judgment by complying with the Sister State Money Judgments Act (CCP §§1710.10–1710.65). *Kahn v Berman* (1988) 198 CA3d 1499, 244 CR 575. The court in *Kahn* rejected the argument that this requirement violated the full faith and credit clause of the United States Constitution.

California's statutory limitations on the recovery of attorney fees incurred in the enforcement of a judgment (CCP §685.040) do not apply to a sister-state judgment awarding such fees. The award of fees in a sister-state judgment is enforceable under the full faith and credit clause. *Aspen Int'l Capital Corp. v Marsch* (1991) 235 CA3d 1199, 286 CR 921. However, in an action to enforce a sister-state judgment based on a contract containing an attorney fees provision, the prevailing party in California may not recover fees under CC §1717. The California action is not a prosecution of the contract but an action to enforce a judgment. *Hambrose Reserve, Ltd. v Faitz* (1992) 9 CA4th 129, 11 CR2d 638.

Application for entry of judgment based on a sister-state judgment must now be filed in municipal or justice court when the sister-state judgment is $25,000 or less. CCP §1710.20(a).

[§6.48] Period of Judgment's Enforceability

Effective January 1, 1994, the Family Law Act (CC §§4000–5317) was repealed and replaced by the Family Code.

Perfecting Judgment Lien

Judgment Lien on Real Property

[§6.50] Lump Sum or Installment Judgment

Under CCP §697.340(a), a judgment lien will not affect previously transferred property. Thus, a recorded abstract of judgment does not attach to real property that has already been conveyed by an unrecorded quitclaim deed. *Casey v Gray* (1993) 13 CA4th 611, 16 CR2d 538.

[§6.51] Judicial Council Form 982(a)(1): Abstract of Judgment

ATTORNEY OR PARTY WITHOUT ATTORNEY *(Name and Address)*: TELEPHONE NO.: FOR RECORDER'S USE ONLY

☐ Recording requested by and return to:

☐ ATTORNEY FOR ☐ JUDGMENT CREDITOR ☐ ASSIGNEE OF RECORD

NAME OF COURT:
STREET ADDRESS:
MAILING ADDRESS:
CITY AND ZIP CODE:
BRANCH NAME:

PLAINTIFF:

DEFENDANT:

CASE NUMBER:

ABSTRACT OF JUDGMENT

FOR COURT USE ONLY

1. The ☐ judgment creditor ☐ assignee of record applies for an abstract of judgment and represents the following:
   a. Judgment debtor's
      Name and last known address
   b. Driver's license No. and state: ☐ Unknown
   c. Social Security No.: ☐ Unknown
   d. Summons or notice of entry of sister-state judgment was personally served or mailed to *(name and address)*:
   e. ☐ Additional judgment debtors are shown on reverse.

Date:

(TYPE OR PRINT NAME) ▶ (SIGNATURE OF APPLICANT OR ATTORNEY)

2. a. ☐ I certify that the following is a true and correct abstract of the judgment entered in this action.
   b. ☐ A certified copy of the judgment is attached.
3. Judgment creditor *(name)*:

   whose **address** appears on this form above the court's name.
4. Judgment debtor *(full name as it appears in judgment)*:

[SEAL]

5. a. Judgment entered on *(date)*:
   b. Renewal entered on *(date)*:
   c. Renewal entered on *(date)*:

This abstract issued on *(date)*:

6. Total amount of judgment as entered or last renewed:
   $
7. ☐ An ☐ execution ☐ attachment lien is endorsed on the judgment as follows:
   a. Amount: $
   b. In favor of *(name and address)*:
8. A stay of enforcement has
   a. ☐ not been ordered by the court.
   b. ☐ been ordered by the court effective until *(date)*:
9. ☐ This judgment is an installment judgment.

Clerk, by ______________________, Deputy

Form Adopted by Rule 982
Judicial Council of California
982(a)(1) [Rev. January 1, 1991]

ABSTRACT OF JUDGMENT (CIVIL)

Code of Civil Procedure, §§ 488.480, 674, 700.190

PLAINTIFF:	CASE NUMBER:
DEFENDANT:	

INFORMATION ON ADDITIONAL JUDGMENT DEBTORS

10. Name and last known address

Driver's license No. & state: ☐ Unknown
Social Security No.: ☐ Unknown
Summons was personally served at or mailed to *(address)*:

11. Name and last known address

Driver's license No. & state: ☐ Unknown
Social Security No.: ☐ Unknown
Summons was personally served at or mailed to *(address)*:

12. Name and last known address

Driver's license No. & state: ☐ Unknown
Social Security No.: ☐ Unknown
Summons was personally served at or mailed to *(address)*:

13. Name and last known address

Driver's license No. & state: ☐ Unknown
Social Security No.: ☐ Unknown
Summons was personally served at or mailed to *(address)*:

14. Name and last known address

Driver's license No. & state: ☐ Unknown
Social Security No.: ☐ Unknown
Summons was personally served at or mailed to *(address)*:

15. Name and last known address

Driver's license No. & state: ☐ Unknown
Social Security No.: ☐ Unknown
Summons was personally served at or mailed to *(address)*:

16. Name and last known address

Driver's license No. & state: ☐ Unknown
Social Security No.: ☐ Unknown
Summons was personally served at or mailed to *(address)*:

17. Name and last known address

Driver's license No. & state: ☐ Unknown
Social Security No.: ☐ Unknown
Summons was personally served at or mailed to *(address)*:

18. ☐ Continued on attachment 18.

982(a)(1) [Rev. January 1, 1991] **ABSTRACT OF JUDGMENT (CIVIL)** Page two

Comment: Counsel should be careful to supply all information required by this Judicial Council form; otherwise, the abstract might be a nullity. In *Keele v Reich* (1985) 169 CA3d 1129, 215 CR 756, the omission of the judgment debtor's social security number when it was known or immediately accessible to the judgment creditor was held to nullify the abstract of judgment. Thus, it is especially important for counsel representing clients who are likely to have such information (e.g., lenders whose loan applications contain social security numbers) to ask their clients to search their records. But see *Commonwealth Land Title Co. v Kornbluth* (1985) 175 CA3d 518, 530, 220 CR 774, which held that, although the date of entry of judgment was omitted from one of five abstracts of judgment simultaneously recorded, the omission was an inadvertent clerical error subject to correction, which did not void the abstract of judgment. The court in *Kornbluth* distinguished the omission in *Keele* by characterizing it as purposeful rather than inadvertent. 175 CA3d at 531 n6.

An abstract of judgment recorded after January 1, 1979, that does not list the judgment debtor's social security number and driver's license number may be corrected by the recording of an amendment containing all the information required by CCP §674 and listing the debtor's driver's license number and social security number if they were known at the time the original abstract of judgment was recorded. The amendment must also specify the date of recording and the book and page location in the records of the county recorder of the original abstract of judgment. A recorded amendment to an abstract of judgment has priority as of the recordation date of the original abstract of judgment, except as to certain specified purchasers, encumbrancers, and lessees without actual notice of the original abstract of judgment. CCP §674(b).

The Judicial Council has promulgated a form for an abstract of judgment ordering a party to pay spousal, child, or family support containing the information required by Fam C §4506. This form is printed in §6.51A.

[§6.51A] Judicial Council Form 1285.80: Abstract of Support Judgment

ATTORNEY OR PARTY WITHOUT ATTORNEY (Name and Address): TELEPHONE NO.: | FOR RECORDER'S USE ONLY

☐ Recording requested by and return to:

☐ ATTORNEY FOR ☐ JUDGMENT CREDITOR ☐ ASSIGNEE OF RECORD

SUPERIOR COURT OF CALIFORNIA, COUNTY OF

STREET ADDRESS:
MAILING ADDRESS:
CITY AND ZIP CODE:
BRANCH NAME:

PETITIONER/PLAINTIFF:

RESPONDENT/DEFENDANT:

ABSTRACT OF SUPPORT JUDGMENT | CASE NUMBER:

FOR COURT USE ONLY

1. The ☐ judgment creditor ☐ assignee of record
applies for an abstract of a support judgment and represents the following:
a. Judgment debtor's
Name and last known address

b. Driver's license No. and state: ☐ unknown
c. Social Security number: ☐ unknown
d. Birthdate: ☐ unknown

Date:

(TYPE OR PRINT NAME) ▶ (SIGNATURE OF APPLICANT OR ATTORNEY)

2. I CERTIFY that the judgment entered in this action contains an order for payment of spousal, family, or child support.
3. Judgment creditor *(name)*:

whose address appears on this form above the court's name.

4. ☐ The support is ordered to be paid to the following county officer *(name and address)*:

5. Judgment debtor *(full name as it appears in judgment)*:

6. a. A judgment was entered on *(date)*:
b. Renewal was entered on *(date)*:
c. Renewal was entered on *(date)*:

7. ☐ An execution lien is endorsed on the judgment as follows:
a. Amount: $
b. In favor of *(name and address)*:

[SEAL]

8. A stay of enforcement has
a. ☐ not been ordered by the court.
b. ☐ been ordered by the court effective until *(date)*:
9. ☐ This is an installment judgment.

This abstract issued on *(date)*:

Clerk, by ________________, Deputy

Form Adopted by Rule 1285.80
Judicial Council of California
1285.80 [Rev. July 1, 1989]

ABSTRACT OF SUPPORT JUDGMENT
(Family Law)

CCP 488.480, 674, 697.320, 700.190

[§6.52] Judgment Lien on Personal Property

Former CCP §117 has been repealed. On the payment of a small claims court judgment in installments, now see CCP §116.620.

Release or Subordination of Judgment Liens Concerning Real Property

[§6.57] Form: Release of Judgment Lien

The following should be substituted for the first sentence in the second paragraph of the form on page 456 in Book §6.57:

This is a release from the judgment lien described herein of all of the interests in real property in __[*name of county*]__ County presently owned or hereafter acquired by the herein-named judgment debtor subject to the lien.

Comment: This change makes the form comply with amendments to CCP §697.370(b)(1).

RENEWAL OF JUDGMENT

[§6.65] In General

The last paragraph of Book §6.65 should be revised to read as follows:

Generally, the renewal provisions of CCP §§683.110–683.220 do not apply to judgments made, entered, or enforceable under the Family Code, or to money judgments against a public entity that is subject to Govt C §965.5 or §970.1. CCP §§683.310–683.320; see Comment to CCP §683.310.

Effective January 1, 1994, the Family Law Act (former CC §§4000–5317) was repealed and replaced by the Family Code.

Notwithstanding any other provision of law, a judgment for child, spousal, or family support, or for reimbursement under Welf & I C §11350, including all interest and penalties, is exempt from any requirement that judgments be renewed. A judgment for child or spousal support, including interest and penalties, is enforceable until paid in full. CCP §683.130(c)(1). The judgment creditor has the option, however, of renewing such judgments if the judgment has not been renewed regarding past due amounts or if five years has elapsed since the last renewal. CCP §683.130(c)(2).

Procedure

[§6.68] Time Limitations; Entry of Judgment

Notwithstanding any other provision of law, a judgment for child, spousal, or family support, or for reimbursement under Welf & I C §11350, including all interest and penalties, is exempt from any requirement that judgments be renewed. A judgment for child or spousal support, including interest and penalties, is enforceable until paid in full. CCP §683.130(c)(1). For further discussion, see Update §6.65.

[§6.69] Service of Notice of Renewal of Judgment

Effective January 1, 1989, CCP §683.160(a) was amended to allow service of the notice of renewal of judgment by first class mail in addition to personal service.

[§6.70] Judicial Council Form EJ-195: Notice of Renewal of Judgment

ATTORNEY OR PARTY WITHOUT ATTORNEY *(Name and Address)*: TELEPHONE NO.: ATTORNEY FOR *(Name)*:	FOR COURT USE ONLY
NAME OF COURT: STREET ADDRESS: MAILING ADDRESS: CITY AND ZIP CODE: BRANCH NAME:	
PLAINTIFF: DEFENDANT:	
NOTICE OF RENEWAL OF JUDGMENT	CASE NUMBER:

TO JUDGMENT DEBTOR *(name)*:

1. **This renewal extends** the period of enforceability of the judgment until 10 years from the date the application for renewal was filed.

2. **If you object** to this renewal, you may make a motion to vacate or modify the renewal with this court.

3. You must make this motion within **30 days** after service of this notice on you.

4. A copy of the *Application for and Renewal of Judgment* is attached *(Cal. Rules of Court, rule 986)*.

Date: Clerk, by ______________________, Deputy

[SEAL]

See CCP 683.160 for information on method of service

Form Approved by the Judicial Council of California EJ-195 [Rev. July 1, 1989]

NOTICE OF RENEWAL OF JUDGMENT

CCP 683.160

SATISFACTION OF JUDGMENT

[§6.74] Filing Acknowledgment of Satisfaction; Time Limitations; Damages

A creditor must be cautious about the kind of property accepted in satisfaction of a judgment. In *Rettner v Shepherd* (1991) 231 CA3d 943, 282 CR 687, the court held that the antideficiency bar of CCP §580d applied when the creditor accepted a note and deed of trust on real property in satisfaction of the judgment.

[§6.75A] Satisfaction of Judgment in Small Claims Court

The judgment debtor has the option of paying the judgment either directly to the judgment creditor or to the court in which the judgment was entered. CCP §116.840(a). To use the latter option, the debtor must pay a fee up to $25, pay the judgment, including any accrued interest and costs, and file a "request to make payment" with the clerk of the court. The clerk then enters satisfaction of the judgment and remits payment to the judgment creditor. CCP §116.860(b). The "request to make payment" must be on the form prescribed by the Judicial Council. CCP §116.860(a). A copy of this form is found at Update §6.75B. On the judgment debtor's compliance with the above procedures, the clerk of the court must notify the creditor that the judgment has been satisfied and must explain how the creditor may obtain the amount paid in satisfaction. CCP §116.860(e).

If the payment is made directly to the judgment creditor or to the creditor's assignee of record, immediately on receipt of payment the creditor or assignee must file with the court an acknowledgment of satisfaction of judgment (see §§6.74–6.75). CCP §116.850(a). The creditor's refusal to file an acknowledgment of satisfaction of judgment, after written demand and without just cause, may result in liability for damages and a $50 penalty. CCP §116.850(b). At the judgment debtor's request, the clerk of the court must enter a satisfaction of judgment if the judgment debtor establishes a rebuttable presumption of full or partial payment under CCP §116.850(d) and complies with the requirements of CCP §116.860(c). CCP §116.850(c).

[§6.75B] Judicial Council Form SC-145: Request To Pay Judgment to Court

Name and Address of Court:

SMALL CLAIMS CASE NO.

PLAINTIFF/DEMANDANTE *(Name and address of each)*:

DEFENDANT/DEMANDADO *(Name and address of each)*:

☐ See attached sheet for additional plaintiffs and defendants.

REQUEST TO PAY JUDGMENT TO COURT

1. **Instead of paying** the judgment directly to the creditor, I want to pay it to the court.
2. Date judgment was entered *(specify)*:
3. **Judgment creditor** ***(the person or business you were ordered to pay)***
   a. Full name:
   b. Address *(use last known)*:
4. **I understand** that the amount of money I must pay to get a satisfaction of judgment is the total of the
   a. principal amount of money the court ordered me to pay,
   b. costs (if awarded by the court),
   c. interest accrued on the judgment,
   d. the court's processing fee, and
   e. other charges the court has added to the judgment. *(The court will calculate the total (see reverse).)*
5. **Partial payment** *(Complete this section if you have ALREADY PAID PART of the judgment.)*
   ☐ I have already paid part of the judgment.
   Amount paid: $ *(check one or both of the boxes below.)*
   a. ☐ by check or money order. *(Attach a copy of both sides of the canceled check or money order.)*
   b. ☐ by cash. *(Attach a copy of the signed, dated cash receipt.)*
6. I understand that if I pay by personal check, satisfaction of judgment will be delayed 30 days.
7. **I request the court** to calculate the total amount required to enter a satisfaction of judgment, and to enter a satisfaction of judgment after I have paid the total amount to the court.

I declare under penalty of perjury under the laws of the State of California that the foregoing is true and correct.

Date:

(TYPE OR PRINT NAME) ▶ (SIGNATURE OF JUDGMENT DEBTOR)

Judgment creditor: See important notice on reverse.

CERTIFICATION	SATISFACTION OF JUDGMENT (for court use only)
I certify that this document is a true and correct copy of the original on file with this court.	(1) ☐ Full satisfaction of judgment entered as to judgment debtor *(name)*: on *(date)*:
(Seal)	(2) ☐ Full satisfaction of judgment NOT entered as requested *(state reason)*:
Clerk, by ______, Deputy	Clerk, by ______, Deputy

(Continued on reverse)

Form Adopted by the Judicial Council of California SC-145 (New January 1, 1990)

REQUEST TO PAY JUDGMENT TO COURT (Small Claims)

Rule 982.7

PLAINTIFF:	CASE NUMBER:
DEFENDANT:	

FOR COURT USE ONLY

1. Judgment entered on *(date)*:

2. **Amount to be paid as of date of request *(specify)*:**
   a. Unpaid principal . . . . $
   b. Costs . . . . $
   c. Post judgment costs . . . . $
   d. Credits *(see receipts)* . . . . $
   e. Interest accrued (to date in item 2, above) . . . . $
   f. Processing fee . . . . $
   g. Other *(specify)* . . . . $

SUBTOTAL $

Add interest at: $ per day *(from date in item 2)* . . . . $

TOTAL $

CLERK'S CERTIFICATE OF MAILING

I certify that I am not a party to this action. This Notice to Judgment Creditor was mailed first class, postage prepaid, in a sealed envelope to the address shown in item 3 on the reverse. The mailing and this certification occurred
at *(place)*: California,
on *(date)*:

Clerk, by ____________________, Deputy

NOTICE TO JUDGMENT CREDITOR

1. The judgment debtor has fully satisfied the judgment entered by making payment to the court in the amount shown above.

2. You may claim this money by
   a. presenting this form in person to the court clerk during regular business hours,
   -OR-
   b. mailing this form to the court.

3. Complete the Judgment Creditor's Request for Funds below.

4. Money not claimed within three years becomes the property of the court *(see Government Code sections 50050–50056)*.

JUDGMENT CREDITOR'S REQUEST FOR FUNDS

I request the court to pay the money to me by mail at my current address *(specify)*:

(Mail or deliver this form to the court clerk. Keep a photocopy for yourself.)

Date:

. . . . ▶ ____________________
(TYPE OR PRINT NAME) (SIGNATURE OF JUDGMENT CREDITOR)

7

Execution; Wage Garnishment

Wage Garnishment

Earnings Withholding Orders Not Involving Collection of Taxes
Procedure
Obtaining Earnings Withholding Order
[§7.65] Judicial Council Form 982.5(1): Application for Earnings Withholding Order
Manner of Levy; Papers Served on Employer
[§7.67] Judicial Council Form 982.5(2): Earnings Withholding Order (With Employer's Instructions).
[§7.68] Judicial Council Form 982.5(3): Earnings Withholding Order for Support (With Employer's Instructions).
[§7.69] Judicial Council Form 982.5(4): Employer's Return
[§7.70] Judicial Council Form 982.5(A): Employee Instructions
Employer's Duties After Being Served With Earnings Withholding Order
[§7.73] Duration of Withholding Period; Payment to Levying Officer
Priority
[§7.75] When Wage Assignment for Support Involved
Earnings Exempt From Withholding
State Exemption
[§7.81] Earnings Withholding Order for Support
Service of Subsequent Earnings Withholding Order by Same Judgment Creditor
[§7.82] Time Limitation
[§7.83] For Recovery of Costs and Interest

EXECUTION

Writ of Execution

[§7.3] Issuance; Limitation

Effective January 1, 1994, the former Family Law Act (former CC §§4000–5317) was repealed and replaced by the Family Code.

[§7.5] Judicial Council Form EJ-130: Writ of Execution

ATTORNEY OR PARTY WITHOUT ATTORNEY *(Name and Address)*: TELEPHONE NO.: FOR RECORDER'S USE ONLY

☐ Recording requested by and return to:

☐ ATTORNEY FOR ☐ JUDGMENT CREDITOR ☐ ASSIGNEE OF RECORD

NAME OF COURT:
STREET ADDRESS:
MAILING ADDRESS:
CITY AND ZIP CODE:
BRANCH NAME:

PLAINTIFF:

DEFENDANT:

WRIT OF ☐ **EXECUTION (Money Judgment)**
☐ **POSSESSION OF** ☐ **Personal Property** ☐ **Real Property**
☐ **SALE**

CASE NUMBER:

FOR COURT USE ONLY

1. **To the Sheriff or any Marshal or Constable of the County of:**

   You are directed to enforce the judgment described below with daily interest and your costs as provided by law.
2. **To any registered process server:** You are authorized to serve this writ only in accord with CCP 699.080 or CCP 715.040.
3. *(Name)*:
   is the ☐ judgment creditor ☐ assignee of record
   whose address is shown on this form above the court's name.
4. **Judgment debtor** *(name and last known address)*:

   ☐ additional judgment debtors on reverse
5. **Judgment entered** on *(date)*:
6. ☐ **Judgment renewed** on *(dates)*:
7. **Notice of sale** under this writ
   a. ☐ has not been requested.
   b. ☐ has been requested *(see reverse)*.
8. ☐ Joint debtor information on reverse.

[SEAL]

9. ☐ See reverse for information on real or personal property to be delivered under a writ of possession or sold under a writ of sale.
10. ☐ This writ is issued on a sister-state judgment.
11. Total judgment . . . . $
12. Costs after judgment (per filed order or memo CCP 685.090) . . . . $
13. Subtotal *(add 11 and 12)* . . . . $
14. Credits . . . . $
15. Subtotal *(subtract 14 from 13)* . . . . . $
16. Interest after judgment (per filed affidavit CCP 685.050) . . . . $
17. Fee for issuance of writ . . . . $
18. **Total** *(add 15, 16, and 17)* . . . . . . $
19. Levying officer:
    (a) Add daily interest from date of writ *(at the legal rate on 15)* of. . . . . . $
    (b) Pay directly to court costs included in 11 and 17 (GC 6103.5, 68511.3; CCP 699.520(i)) . . . . $
20. ☐ The amounts called for in items 11-19 are different for each debtor. These amounts are stated for each debtor on Attachment 20.

Issued on *(date)*: Clerk, by ____________________, Deputy

— NOTICE TO PERSON SERVED: SEE REVERSE FOR IMPORTANT INFORMATION. —

(Continued on reverse)

Form Approved by the Judicial Council of California
EJ-130 [Rev. January 1, 1997*]

WRIT OF EXECUTION

Code of Civil Procedure, §§ 699.520, 712.010, 715.010
* See note on reverse

SHORT TITLE:	CASE NUMBER:

— Items continued from the first page —

4. ☐ **Additional judgment debtor** *(name and last known address)*:

7. ☐ **Notice of sale** has been requested by *(name and address)*:

8. ☐ **Joint debtor** was declared bound by the judgment (CCP 989-994)

a. on *(date)*:
b. name and address of joint debtor:

a. on *(date)*:
b. name and address of joint debtor:

c. ☐ additional costs against certain joint debtors *(itemize)*:

9. ☐ *(Writ of Possession or Writ of Sale)* **Judgment** was entered for the following:
   a. ☐ Possession of real property: The complaint was filed on *(date)*: ***(Check (1) or (2))***:
      (1) ☐ The Prejudgment Claim of Right to Possession was served in compliance with CCP 415.46. The judgment includes all tenants, subtenants, named claimants, and other occupants of the premises.
      (2) ☐ The Prejudgment Claim of Right to Possession was NOT served in compliance with CCP 415.46.
         (a) $ was the daily rental value on the date the complaint was filed.
         (b) The court will hear objections to enforcement of the judgment under CCP 1174.3 on the following dates *(specify)*:
   b. ☐ Possession of personal property
      ☐ If delivery cannot be had, then for the value *(itemize in 9e)* specified in the judgment or supplemental order.
   c. ☐ Sale of personal property
   d. ☐ Sale of real property
   e. Description of property:

— NOTICE TO PERSON SERVED —

WRIT OF EXECUTION OR SALE. Your rights and duties are indicated on the accompanying Notice of Levy.
WRIT OF POSSESSION OF PERSONAL PROPERTY. If the levying officer is not able to take custody of the property, the levying officer will make a demand upon you for the property. If custody is not obtained following demand, the judgment may be enforced as a money judgment for the value of the property specified in the judgment or in a supplemental order.
WRIT OF POSSESSION OF REAL PROPERTY. If the premises are not vacated within five days after the date of service on the occupant or, if service is by posting, within five days after service on you, the levying officer will remove the occupants from the real property and place the judgment creditor in possession of the property. Except for a mobile home, personal property remaining on the premises will be sold or otherwise disposed of in accordance with CCP 1174 unless you or the owner of the property pays the judgment creditor the reasonable cost of storage and takes possession of the personal property not later than 15 days after the time the judgment creditor takes possession of the premises.
► *A Claim of Right to Possession form accompanies this writ (unless the Summons was served in compliance with CCP 415.46).*

* NOTE: Continued use of form EJ-130 (Rev. July 1, 1996) is authorized through December 31, 1997.

Executing Writ

[§7.11] Judicial Council Form EJ-155: Exemptions From Enforcement of Judgment

On the possible conflict between state exemption statutes and federal law, see Update §9.6.

What Property May Be Levied on Under Writ of Execution

[§7.13] By Levying Officer; Property Subject to Enforcement of Money Judgment Generally

"Levying officer" is now defined as the sheriff or marshal. CCP §680.260.

If property subject to a lien created under CCP §§695.010–709.030 remains subject to the lien after the property is transferred or otherwise encumbered, the money judgment may be enforced against the property in the same manner and to the same extent as if it had not been transferred or encumbered. CCP §695.070(a). If the judgment debtor dies after the transfer of property subject to the lien, the money judgment may still be enforced against the property, as in CCP §695.070(a). CCP §695.070(b).

On the possible conflict between state exemption statutes and federal law, see Update §9.6.

For the subject matter of former Com C §8317, now see Com C §8112.

[§7.17] Return of Writ of Execution; Time Limitations

If a levy has been made under the Wage Garnishment Law (CCP §§706.010–706.154) and the earnings withholding order remains in effect, the writ of execution must now be returned as provided in CCP §699.560(a). CCP §699.560(d). If the writ is returned before the earnings withholding order terminates, on termination of the earnings withholding order, the levying officer must make a supplemental return on the writ. The supplemental return must contain the same information as the original return under CCP §699.560. CCP §§699.560(d), 706.033.

Levy on Particular Types of Personal Property

[§7.23] Going Business; Keepers

Effective January 1, 1997, when a keeper is placed in a business for the purpose of taking into custody tangible personal property consisting solely of money or equivalent proceeds of sales, the levying officer is authorized to take the property into exclusive custody at the end of each daily keeper period. CCP §700.070(c). This is an exception to the rule in CCP §700.070(b)(1)–(3) regarding when the levying officer is to take tangible personal property into custody (*i.e.,* when the judgment debtor objects, when the judgment creditor so requests, or at the end of ten days from the time the keeper is placed in charge of the business).

California State Sheriffs' Association Civil Procedure Manual (3d ed rev 1978) has been replaced by California State Sheriffs' Association Civil Procedural Manual (4th ed rev 1994).

[§7.24] Sample San Francisco Sheriff's Form: Keeper Instructions—8 Hours

1 2 3 4 5 6 7

______________ Sheriff's File No.

IN THE ______________________ COURT,
CITY AND COUNTY OF SAN FRANCISCO

______________________)
Plaintiff)
)
vs.) Court Case No. ______________
)
)
______________________)
Defendant

TO THE SHERIFF OF THE CITY AND COUNTY OF SAN FRANCISCO:

You are hereby instructed to garnish the above named defendant's

☐ Bank Account (Account No. if known) ______________________

☐ Other: ______________________

by virtue of the accompanying Writ of Execution (Money Judgement) all monies, debts, credits and effects due or owing Defendant (Judgment Debtor) cited above in possession or under the control of the following persons, firms or corporations:

____
Specific Name of Institution

____
Specific Street Address

San Francisco, California ZIP ______

Date, San Francisco, ______________________, 1989

____
Plaintiff or Plaintiff's Attorney

Address: ______________________

City: ______________________

Day Telephone: ______________________

F2729, Rev. 9/88

[§7.27] Personal Property Used as a Dwelling

Code of Civil Procedure §700.080 has been amended to provide that personal property used as a dwelling includes a mobilehome, whether the mobilehome is occupied or unoccupied at the time of the levy. CCP §700.080(d).

[§7.31A] Lottery Prizes

A new CCP §708.755 (former CCP §708.750) has been added to provide for a judgment lien against a lottery prize to be paid in annual installments. Once created, the lien continues in force and effect until the judgment is paid or expires. The judgment creditor must file annually an affidavit with the lottery stating that the judgment has not been satisfied and the amount of the remaining unsatisfied judgment. The lien expires on failure to file the affidavit. (Code of Civil Procedure §708.750 as discussed in Book §§8.66–8.68 remains in effect.)

Third Person's (Garnishee's) Duties and Liabilities After Levy

[§7.35] Secured Party

Code of Civil Procedure §701.040(b) has been amended to provide that, after the security interest is satisfied, the secured party must deliver any excess property and pay any excess payments or proceeds to the levying officer for the purpose of the levy as provided in Com C §9504 unless the court or the levying officer directs otherwise.

Levy on Real Property; Sale

Homesteads

[§7.42] Homestead Exemption; Amount

Code of Civil Procedure §704.730(a)(2) has been amended to increase the homestead exemption to $75,000 if the judgment debtor or his or her spouse who resides in the homestead is, at the time of the attempted sale, a member of a family unit and there is at least one member of the family unit who owns no interest in the homestead or whose only interest in the homestead is a community property interest with the judgment debtor.

Code of Civil Procedure §704.730(a)(3) has been amended to increase the homestead exemption to $100,000 if the judgment debtor or his or her spouse who resides in the homestead is, at the time of the attempted sale, either 65 years of age or older, or physically or mentally disabled. This exemption also applies to persons 55 years of age or older with a gross annual income of not more than $15,000 or, if the judgment debtor is married, a gross annual income, including the gross annual income of the judgment debtor's spouse, of not more than $20,000, when the sale is an involuntary sale.

Code of Civil Procedure §704.730(a)(1) has been amended to increase the homestead exemption to $50,000 unless the judgment debtor, or his or her spouse who resides in the homestead, is a person described in CCP §704.730(a)(2) or (3).

The amount of the homestead exemption is determined at the time that a judgment lien is obtained, not at the time the levy of execution is made on the property. CCP §703.050(a); *Berhanu v Metzger* (1992) 12 CA4th 445, 15 CR2d 191. Thus, the homestead exemption in *Berhanu* was $45,000 rather than $75,000, because the abstract of judgment was recorded on December 18, 1990, before the exemption was increased on January 1, 1991.

Procedure To Obtain Order; Sale

[§7.51] Court Determination; Order of Sale

Code of Civil Procedure §704.780(b) has been amended to provide that a court not make an order for sale of a dwelling subject to a homestead exemption if it determines that the sale would not be likely to produce a bid sufficient to satisfy any part of the amount due on the judgment.

[§7.54] Limitation on Sale

Under CCP §704.800(a), the forced sale of a homestead is not permitted unless a bid is received that is greater than the amount of the homestead exemption "plus any additional amount necessary to satisfy all liens and encumbrances on the property." In *In re Hyman* (Hyman v Plotkin) (9th Cir 1992) 967 F2d 1316, 1320, the court held that selling costs are not included in the calculation of this amount. The court rejected the homeowners' contention that the bankruptcy trustee could not sell their home because the exemption plus all liens and encumbrances and selling costs would exceed the selling price of the house. The court also rejected the contention that the homeowner is entitled to any appreciation in the property's value between the filing of the bankruptcy petition and the time of sale. The exemption does not provide for an equity interest subject to appreciation or depreciation. 967 F2d at 1321.

Debtor's Remedies Against Execution

Stay of Execution

[§7.56] Statutory Authority

Former CCP §117.7 has been repealed and replaced in relevant part by CCP §116.810.

[§7.57] Execution of Enforcement Liens; Exceptions

Effective January 1, 1994, former CCP §1699 was repealed and replaced by Fam C §4853, which is substantially the same.

Remedies After Execution Sale

[§7.62] Setting Aside Improper Execution Sale; Damages

When the purchaser at an execution sale is the judgment creditor, the time within which the judgment debtor or the judgment debtor's successor in interest may commence an action to set aside the sale is now 90 days. CCP §701.680(c)(1). If the sale is set aside, any liens extinguished by the sale of the property are revived and reattach to the property with the same priority and effect as if the sale had not been made. CCP §701.680(c)(1).

WAGE GARNISHMENT

Earnings Withholding Orders Not Involving Collection of Taxes

Procedure

Obtaining Earnings Withholding Order

[§7.65] Judicial Council Form 982.5(1): Application for Earnings Withholding Order

ATTORNEY OR PARTY WITHOUT ATTORNEY *(Name and Address)*: TELEPHONE NO.:	LEVYING OFFICER *(Name and Address)*:	
ATTORNEY FOR *(Name)*:		
NAME OF COURT, JUDICIAL DISTRICT OR BRANCH COURT, IF ANY:		
PLAINTIFF: DEFENDANT:		
APPLICATION FOR EARNINGS WITHHOLDING ORDER **(Wage Garnishment)**	LEVYING OFFICER FILE NO.:	COURT CASE NO.:

TO THE SHERIFF OR ANY MARSHAL OR CONSTABLE OF THE COUNTY OF
OR ANY REGISTERED PROCESS SERVER

1. The judgment creditor *(name)*:

requests issuance of an Earnings Withholding Order directing the employer to withhold the earnings of the judgment debtor (employee).

Name and address of employer

Name and address of employee

Social Security Number *(if known)*:

2. The amounts withheld are to be paid to
   a. ☐ The attorney (or party without an attorney) named at the top of this page.
   b. ☐ Other *(name, address, and telephone)*:

3. a. Judgment was entered on *(date)*:
   b. Collect the amount directed by the Writ of Execution unless a lesser amount is specified here:
   $

4. ☐ The Writ of Execution was issued to collect delinquent amounts payable for the **support** of a child, former spouse, or spouse of the employee.

5. ☐ Special Instructions *(specify)*:

6. ***(Check a or b)***
   a. ☐ I have not previously obtained an order directing this employer to withhold the earnings of this employee.
   —OR—
   b. ☐ I have previously obtained such an order, but that order *(check one)*:
      ☐ was terminated by a court order, but I am entitled to apply for another Earnings Withholding Order under the provisions of Code of Civil Procedure section 706.105(h).
      ☐ was ineffective.

.... ▶ ____________________
(TYPE OR PRINT NAME) *(SIGNATURE OF ATTORNEY OR PARTY WITHOUT ATTORNEY)*

I declare under penalty of perjury under the laws of the State of California that the foregoing is true and correct.

Date:

.... ▶ ____________________
(TYPE OR PRINT NAME) *(SIGNATURE OF DECLARANT)*

Form Adopted by the Judicial Council of California 982.5(1) [Rev. January 1, 1993]

APPLICATION FOR EARNINGS WITHHOLDING ORDER
(Wage Garnishment)

CCP 706.121

Manner of Levy; Papers Served on Employer

[§7.67] Judicial Council Form 982.5(2): Earnings Withholding Order (With Employer's Instructions)

982.5(2)

ATTORNEY OR PARTY WITHOUT ATTORNEY *(Name, state bar number, and address)*	TELEPHONE AND FAX NOS	LEVYING OFFICER *(Name and address)*
ATTORNEY FOR *(Name)*		
NAME OF COURT, JUDICIAL DISTRICT AND BRANCH COURT, IF ANY		
PLAINTIFF:		
DEFENDANT:		
EARNINGS WITHHOLDING ORDER (Wage Garnishment)	LEVYING OFFICER FILE NO	COURT CASE NO

EMPLOYEE: *KEEP YOUR COPY OF THIS LEGAL PAPER.* ***EMPLEADO:*** *GUARDE ESTE PAPEL OFICIAL.*

EMPLOYER: ***Enter the following date to assist your record keeping.***

Date this order was received by employer *(specify the date of personal delivery by levying officer or registered process server or the date mail receipt was signed)*:

TO THE EMPLOYER REGARDING YOUR EMPLOYEE:

Name and address of employer

Name and address of employee

Social Security Number *(if known)*

1. A judgment creditor has obtained this order to collect a court judgment against your employee. You are directed to withhold part of the earnings of the employee *(see instructions on reverse of this form)*. Pay the withheld sums to the **levying officer** *(name and address above)*.

   If the employee works for you now, you must **give the employee a copy of this order** and the ***Employee Instructions*** (form 982.5(A)) within 10 days after receiving this order.

   Complete both copies of the *Employer's Return* (form 982.5(4)) **and mail them to the levying officer** within 15 days after receiving this order, whether or not the employee works for you.

2. The total amount due is: $

   Count 10 calendar days from the date when you received this order. If your employee's pay period ends before the tenth day, ***do not*** withhold earnings payable for that pay period. *Do* withhold from earnings that are payable for any pay period ending on or after that tenth day.

   Continue withholding for all pay periods until you withhold the amount due. The levying officer will notify you of an assessment you should withhold in addition to the amount due. Do not withhold more than the total of these amounts. Never withhold any earnings payable before the beginning of the earnings withholding period.

3. The judgment was entered in the court on *(date)*:

   The judgment creditor *(if different from the plaintiff)* is *(name)*:

4. The *Employer's Instructions* on the reverse tell you how much of the employee's earnings to withhold each payday and answer other questions you may have.

Date:

(TYPE OR PRINT NAME) ▶ (SIGNATURE)

☐ LEVYING OFFICER ☐ REGISTERED PROCESS SERVER

(Employer's Instructions on reverse)

Form Adopted by the Judicial Council of California 982.5(2) [Rev. September 1, 1997]

EARNINGS WITHHOLDING ORDER (Wage Garnishment)

Code of Civil Procedure, §§ 706.022, 706.108, 706.125

EMPLOYER'S INSTRUCTIONS

EARNINGS WITHHOLDING ORDERS

The instructions in paragraph 1 on the reverse of this form describe your early duties to provide information to your employee and the levying officer.

Your other duties are TO WITHHOLD THE CORRECT AMOUNT OF EARNINGS (if any) and PAY IT TO THE LEVYING OFFICER during the *withholding period*.

The withholding period is the period covered by the *Earnings Withholding Order* (this order). The withholding period begins ten (10) calendar days after you receive the order and continues until the total amount due, plus additional amounts for costs and interest (which will be listed in a levying officer's notice), is withheld.

It may end sooner if (1) you receive a written notice signed by the levying officer specifying an earlier termination date, or (2) an order of higher priority (explained on the reverse of the *Employer's Return*) is received.

You are entitled to rely on and must obey all written notices signed by the levying officer.

The *Employer's Return* (form 982.5(4)) describes several situations that could affect the withholding period for this order. If you receive more than one *Earnings Withholding Order* during a withholding period, review that form (*Employer's Return*) for instructions.

If the employee stops working for you, the *Earnings Withholding Order* ends after no amounts are withheld for a continuous 180 day period. If withholding ends because the earnings are subject to an order of higher priority, the *Earnings Withholding Order* ends after a continuous two year period during which no amounts are withheld under the order. **Return the *Earnings Withholding Order* to the levying officer with a statement of the reason it is being returned.**

WHAT TO DO WITH THE MONEY

The amounts withheld during the withholding period must be paid to the levying officer by the 15th of the next month after each payday. If you wish to pay more frequently than monthly, each payment must be made within ten (10) days after the close of the pay period.

Be sure to mark each check with the case number, the levying officer's file number, if different, and the employee's name so the money will be applied to the correct account.

WHAT IF YOU STILL HAVE QUESTIONS?

The garnishment law is contained in the Code of Civil Procedure beginning with section 706.010. Sections 706.022, 706.025, and 706.104 explain the employer's duties.

The Federal Wage Garnishment Law and federal rules provide the basic protections on which the California law is based. Inquiries about the federal law will be answered by mail, telephone, or personal interview at any office of the Wage and Hour Division of the U.S. Department of Labor. Offices are listed in the telephone directory under the U.S. Department of Labor in the U.S. Government listing.

THE CHART BELOW AND THESE INSTRUCTIONS DO NOT APPLY TO ORDERS FOR THE SUPPORT OF A SPOUSE, FORMER SPOUSE, OR CHILD.

The chart below shows *HOW MUCH TO WITHHOLD* when the federal minimum wage is $5.15 per hour.
If the *FEDERAL* minimum wage changes in the future, the levying officer will provide a chart showing the new withholding rates.

COMPUTATION INSTRUCTIONS

State and federal law limits the amount of earnings that can be withheld. The limitations are based on the employee's disposable earnings, which are different from gross pay or take-home pay.

To determine the CORRECT AMOUNT OF EARNINGS TO BE WITHHELD (if any), compute the employee's *disposable earnings*.

(A) Earnings include any money (whether called wages, salary, commissions, bonuses, or anything else) that is paid by an employer to an employee for personal services. Vacation or sick pay is subject to withholding as it is received by the employee. Tips are generally not included as earnings since they are not paid by the employer.

(B) *Disposable earnings* are the earnings left after subtracting the part of the earnings a state or federal law requires an employer to withhold. Generally these required deductions are (1) federal income tax, (2) federal social security, (3) state income tax, (4) state disability insurance, and (5) payments to public employee retirement systems. Disposable earnings will change when the required deductions change.

After the employee's *disposable earnings* are known, use the chart below to determine what amount should be withheld. In the column listed under the employee's pay period, find the employee's disposable earnings. The amount shown below that is the amount to be withheld. For example, if the employee is paid disposable earnings of $500 twice a month (semi-monthly), the correct amount to withhold is 25 percent each payday, or $125.

The chart below is based on the minimum wage that was effective September 1, 1997. It will change if the minimum wage changes. Restrictions are based on the minimum wage effective at the time the earnings are payable.

Occasionally, the employee's earnings will also be subject to a *Wage and Earnings Assignment Order*, an order available from family law courts for child, spousal, or family support. The amount required to be withheld for that order should be deducted from the amount to be withheld for this order.

—IMPORTANT WARNINGS—

1. IT IS AGAINST THE LAW TO FIRE THE EMPLOYEE BECAUSE OF *EARNINGS WITHHOLDING ORDERS* FOR THE PAYMENT OF ONLY ONE INDEBTEDNESS. No matter how many orders you receive, so long as they all relate to a single indebtedness (no matter how many debts are represented in that judgment) the employee may not be fired.
2. IT IS ILLEGAL TO AVOID AN *EARNINGS WITHHOLDING ORDER* BY POSTPONING OR ADVANCING THE PAYMENT OF EARNINGS. The employee's pay period must not be changed to prevent the order from taking effect.
3. IT IS ILLEGAL NOT TO PAY AMOUNTS WITHHELD FOR THE *EARNINGS WITHHOLDING ORDER* TO THE LEVYING OFFICER. Your duty is to pay the money to the levying officer who will pay the money in accordance with the laws that apply to this case.

IF YOU VIOLATE ANY OF THESE LAWS, YOU MAY BE HELD LIABLE TO PAY CIVIL DAMAGES AND YOU MAY BE SUBJECT TO CRIMINAL PROSECUTION!

FEDERAL MINIMUM WAGE: $5.15 per hour **(Beginning September 1, 1997, and continuing indefinitely.)**

PAY PERIOD	Daily	Weekly	Every Two Weeks	Twice a Month	Monthly
DISPOSABLE EARNINGS	$0-$154.50	$0-$154.50	$0-$309.00	$0-$334.75	$0-$669.50
Withhold	None	None	None	None	None
DISPOSABLE EARNINGS	$154.51-$206.00	$154.51-$206.00	$309.01-$412.00	$334.76-$446.33	$669.51-$892.67
Withhold	Amount above $154.50	Amount above $154.50	Amount above $309.00	Amount above $334.75	Amount above $669.50
DISPOSABLE EARNINGS	$206.01 or More	$206.01 or More	$412.01 or More	$446.34 or More	$892.68 or More
Withhold	Maximum of 25% of Disposable Earnings	Maximum of 25% of Disposable Earnings	Maximum of 25% of Disposable Earnings	Maximum of 25% of Disposable Earnings	Maximum of 25% of Disposable Earnings

[§7.68] Judicial Council Form 982.5(3): Earnings Withholding Order for Support (With Employer's Instructions)

ATTORNEY OR PARTY WITHOUT ATTORNEY *(Name and Address)*: TELEPHONE NO.:	LEVYING OFFICER *(Name and Address)*:
ATTORNEY FOR *(Name)*:	
NAME OF COURT, JUDICIAL DISTRICT OR BRANCH COURT, IF ANY:	
PLAINTIFF: DEFENDANT:	
EARNINGS WITHHOLDING ORDER FOR SUPPORT **(Wage Garnishment)**	LEVYING OFFICER FILE NO.: / COURT CASE NO.:

EMPLOYEE: *KEEP YOUR COPY OF THIS LEGAL PAPER.* ***EMPLEADO:*** *GUARDE ESTE PAPEL OFICIAL.*

EMPLOYER: ***Enter the following date to assist your record keeping.***

Date this order was received by employer ***(specify the date of personal delivery by levying officer or registered process server or the date mail receipt was signed):***

TO THE EMPLOYER REGARDING YOUR EMPLOYEE:

Name and address of employer

Name and address of employee

Social Security Number *(if known)*:

1. A judgment creditor has obtained this order to collect a court judgment against your employee. You are directed to withhold part of the earnings of the employee *(see instructions on reverse of this form)*. Pay the withheld sums to the **levying officer** *(name and address above)*.

   If the employee works for you now, you must **give the employee a copy of this order and the Employee Instructions** within 10 days after receiving this order.

   Complete both copies of the form Employer's Return and **mail them to the levying officer** within 15 days after receiving this order, whether or not the employee works for you.

2. The total amount due is $

   Count 10 calendar days from the date when you received this order. If your employee's pay period ends before the tenth day, ***do not*** withhold earnings payable for that pay period. ***Do*** withhold from earnings that are payable for the pay period ending on or after that tenth day.

   Continue withholding until
   (1) the total amount due has been withheld; or
   (2) you receive a court order or an order from the levying officer telling you to stop the withholding earlier.

3. The judgment was entered in the court shown above. The judgment creditor is *(name)*:

4. The EMPLOYER'S INSTRUCTIONS on the reverse tell you how much of the employee's earnings to withhold each payday. Follow those instructions unless you receive a court order or order from the levying officer giving you other instructions.

Date:

(TYPE OR PRINT NAME) *(SIGNATURE)*

☐ *LEVYING OFFICER* ☐ *REGISTERED PROCESS SERVER*

The EMPLOYER'S INSTRUCTIONS on the reverse contain special rules that apply to Earnings Withholding Order For Support. Read the instructions carefully.

(Employer's Instructions on reverse)

Form Adopted by the Judicial Council of California 982.5(3) [Rev. January 1, 1993]

EARNINGS WITHHOLDING ORDER FOR SUPPORT
(Wage Garnishment)

CCP 706.030
706.052
706.108

EMPLOYER'S INSTRUCTIONS
(EARNINGS WITHHOLDING ORDERS FOR SUPPORT)

These instructions apply *only* to Earnings Withholding Orders for Support. Applicable instructions appear on the reverse of the other types of Earnings Withholding Orders.

The instructions in paragraph 1 on the reverse of this form describe your early duties to provide information to your employee and the levying officer.

Your other duties are TO WITHHOLD THE CORRECT AMOUNT OF EARNINGS (if any) and PAY IT TO THE LEVYING OFFICER during the *withholding period.*

The usual *withholding period* begins ten (10) calendar days after you receive the Earnings Withholding Order. In the case of an Earnings Withholding Order for Support (this order) the *withholding period* continues until one of two things happens: (1) the total amount specified in the order, plus any amounts listed in a notice from the levying officer, has been withheld, or (2) you receive a court order or notice signed by the levying officer specifying a termination date.

You are entitled to rely on and should obey all written notices signed by the levying officer.

The form Employer's Return describes several situations that could affect the withholding period for this order. If you receive more than one Earnings Withholding Order during a withholding period, review that form (Employer's Return) for instructions.

Your duty to withhold does not end merely because the employee no longer works for you. Withholding for an Earnings Withholding Order for Support does not automatically terminate until one year after the employment of the employee by the employer ends.

WHAT TO DO WITH THE MONEY

The amounts withheld during the withholding period must be paid to the levying officer by the 15th of the next month after each payday. If you wish to pay more frequently than monthly, each payment must be made within ten (10) days after the close of the pay period.

Be sure to mark each check with the case number, the levying officer's file number, if different, and the employee's name so the money will be applied to the correct account.

WHAT IF YOU STILL HAVE QUESTIONS?

The garnishment law is contained in the Code of Civil Procedure beginning with section 706.010. Sections 706.022, 706.025, and 706.104 explain the employer's duties.

The Federal Wage Garnishment Law and federal rules provide the basic protections on which the California law is based. Inquiries about the federal law will be answered by mail, telephone, or personal interview at any office of the Wage and Hour Division of the U.S. Department of Labor. Offices are listed in the telephone directory under the U.S. Department of Labor in the U.S. Government listing.

COMPUTATION INSTRUCTIONS

State and federal law limits the amount of earnings that can be withheld. The limitations are based on the employee's disposable earnings, which are different from gross pay or take-home pay.

To determine the CORRECT AMOUNT OF EARNINGS TO BE WITHHELD (if any), compute the employee's *disposable earnings.*

(A) Earnings include any money (whether called wages, salary, commissions, bonuses, or anything else) that is paid by an employer to an employee for personal services. Vacation or sick pay is subject to withholding as it is received by the employee. Tips are generally not included as earnings since they are not paid by the employer.

(B) *Disposable earnings* are the earnings left after subtracting the part of the earnings a state or federal law requires an employer to withhold. Generally these required deductions are (1) federal income tax, (2) federal social security, (3) state income tax, (4) state disability insurance, and (5) payments to public employees' retirement systems. Disposable earnings will change when the required deductions change.

After the employee's disposable earnings are known, WITHHOLD FIFTY (50) PERCENT of the *disposable earnings* for the Withholding Order for Support. For example, if the employee has monthly disposable earnings of $1,432, the sum of $716 would be withheld to pay to the levying officer on account of this order.

Occasionally, the employee's earnings will also be subject to a Wage and Earnings Assignment Order, an order available for child support or spousal support. The amount required to be withheld for that order should be deducted from the amount to be withheld for this order. For example, if the employee is subject to a Wage and Earnings Assignment Order and the employer is required to withhold $300 per month to pay on that order, when the employer receives this Earnings Withholding Order for Support, the employer should deduct the $300 for the Wage and Earnings Assignment Order from the $716 and pay the balance to the levying officer each month for this order.

—IMPORTANT WARNINGS—

1. IT IS AGAINST THE LAW TO FIRE THE EMPLOYEE BECAUSE OF EARNINGS WITHHOLDING ORDERS FOR THE PAYMENT OF ONLY ONE INDEBTEDNESS. No matter how many orders you receive, so long as they all relate to a single judgment (no matter how many debts are represented in that judgment) the employee may not be fired.

2. IT IS ILLEGAL TO AVOID AN EARNINGS WITHHOLDING ORDER BY POSTPONING OR ADVANCING THE PAYMENT OF EARNINGS. The employee's pay period must not be changed to prevent the order from taking effect.

3. IT IS ILLEGAL NOT TO PAY AMOUNTS WITHHELD FOR THE EARNINGS WITHHOLDING ORDER TO THE LEVYING OFFICER. Your duty is to pay the money to the levying officer who will pay the money in accordance with the laws that apply to this case.

IF YOU VIOLATE ANY OF THESE LAWS, YOU MAY BE HELD LIABLE TO PAY CIVIL DAMAGES AND YOU MAY BE SUBJECT TO CRIMINAL PROSECUTION!

[§7.69] Judicial Council Form 982.5(4): Employer's Return

ATTORNEY OR PARTY WITHOUT ATTORNEY *(Name and Address)*: TELEPHONE NO.: ATTORNEY FOR *(Name)*:	LEVYING OFFICER *(Name and Address)*:	
NAME OF COURT, JUDICIAL DISTRICT OR BRANCH COURT, IF ANY:		
PLAINTIFF: DEFENDANT:		
EMPLOYER'S RETURN **(Wage Garnishment)**	LEVYING OFFICER FILE NO.:	COURT CASE NO.:

EMPLOYER: **You must complete both copies of this form and mail them to the levying officer within 15 days. *Please correct any errors* in the mailing information above and provide any missing information, including the name of the person to whom notices should be directed.**

FAILURE TO COMPLETE AND RETURN THESE FORMS MAY SUBJECT YOU TO PAYMENT OF ATTORNEY FEES AND OTHER CIVIL PENALTIES.

Name and address of employer ***Name and address of employee***

Attn: *(Insert name above)* ***Social Security Number*** *(if known)*:

1. I received the Earnings Withholding Order on *(date)*:

2. The employee is
   a. ☐ not employed by this employer *(if not employed, omit items 2b through 6 and proceed to item 7 on reverse)*.
   b. ☐ now employed by this employer and in the last pay period had gross earnings of $

3. The employee's pay period is
   a. ☐ daily b. ☐ weekly c. ☐ every two weeks
   d. ☐ twice a month e. ☐ monthly f. ☐ other *(specify)*:

(IF YOU HAVE RECEIVED NO OTHER ORDERS THAT PRESENTLY AFFECT THIS EMPLOYEE'S EARNINGS, OMIT ITEMS 4, 5, AND 6, AND PROCEED TO ITEM 7 ON REVERSE.)

(Continued on reverse)

SHORT TITLE:	LEVYING OFFICER FILE NO.:	COURT CASE NO.:

If you have received other orders that presently affect this employee's earnings, another order may have priority over this one. The following list indicates the priority of orders:

Wage and Earnings **Assignment** Order (For Support)	First priority
Earnings Withholding Order for Support	Second priority
Earnings Withholding Order for Taxes	Third priority
Earnings Withholding Order	Fourth priority

If two or more orders have the same priority, comply with the one received first. If both were received on the same date, comply with the one with the earlier date of judgment. If the dates of judgment are the same, you may select which order you choose to comply with.

4. ☐ This order appears to have higher priority than any other order. Earnings will be withheld for this order in accord with the EMPLOYER'S INSTRUCTIONS *(on reverse of Earnings Witholding Order).*

5. ☐ The employer has received another order affecting the employee's earnings and earnings are being withheld for the other order because:
   a. ☐ The other order was received first. The other order was received on *(date)*:

   b. ☐ This order does not have higher priority.

   c. ☐ A copy of the other order is attached *(retain original for your records. If a copy is not attached, complete item d.)*

   d. ☐ A copy of the other order is NOT attached. *Describe the other order by providing the following information:*
      (1) Court name, address, and case number:

      (2) Levying officer name, address, and file number:

      (3) Total amount to be withheld: $

6 ☐ This order is not effective for the reason shown in item 5. It is returned to the levying officer with this return.

7. I declare under penalty of perjury under the laws of the State of California that the foregoing is true and correct.

Date:

. . . .
(TYPE OR PRINT NAME)

▶ ____________________________________
(SIGNATURE OF DECLARANT)

If an Earnings Withholding Order is not effective when served, for any reason, do not hold it. Return it to the levying officer with this return.

FAILURE TO COMPLETE AND RETURN THIS FORM MAY SUBJECT AN EMPLOYER TO CIVIL LIABILITY AND ATTORNEY FEES.

[§7.70] Judicial Council Form 982.5(A): Employee Instructions

EMPLOYEE INSTRUCTIONS

—NOTICE—

IMPORTANT LEGAL NOTICE TO EMPLOYEE
ABOUT EARNINGS WITHHOLDING ORDERS
(Wage Garnishment)

The **Earnings Withholding Order** requires your employer to pay part of your earnings to the sheriff or other levying officer. The levying officer will pay the money to a creditor who has a court judgment against you. The information below may help you protect the money you earn.

—NOTICIA—

NOTICIA LEGAL IMPORTANTE RESPECTO
A LAS ORDENES DE RETENCION DE SUELDO

El **Orden de Retención de Sueldo** requiere que su empleador pagé una parte de su sueldo a un oficial de retención. El oficial le pagará el dinero retenido a su acreedor que ha consiguido una decisión judicial en contra de Ud. Pida Ud. que un amigo o su abogado le lea este papel oficial. Esta información le podria ayudar a proteger su sueldo.

CAN YOU BE FIRED BECAUSE OF THIS?

NO. You cannot be fired unless your earnings have been withheld before for a different court judgment. If this is the first judgment for which you wages will be withheld and your employer fires you because of this, the California Labor Commissioner, listed in the phone book of larger cities, can help you get your job back.

HOW MUCH OF YOUR PAY WILL BE WITHHELD?

The reverse of the Earnings Withholding Order (abbreviated in this notice as **EWO**) that applies to you contains Employer Instructions. These explain how much of your earnings can be withheld. Generally, the amount is about 25% of your take home pay until the amount due has been withheld. The levying officer will notify the employee of an additional assessment charged for paying out money collected under this order and that amount will also be withheld.

If you have trouble figuring this out, ask your employer for help.

IS THERE ANYTHING YOU CAN DO?

YES. There are several possibilities.

1. See an attorney. If you do not know an attorney, check with the lawyer referral service or the legal aid office in your county (both are listed in the yellow pages under "Attorneys").

   An attorney may be able to help you make an agreement with your creditor, or may be able to help you stop your earnings from being withheld. You may wish to consider bankruptcy or asking the bankruptcy court to help you pay your creditors. These possibilities may stop your wages from being withheld.

   An attorney can help you decide what is best for you. Take your **EWO** to the attorney to help you get the best advice and the fastest help.

2. Try to work out an agreement yourself with your creditor. Call the creditor or the creditor's attorney, listed on the **EWO**. If you make an agreement, the withholding of your wages will stop or be changed to a smaller amount you agree on. *(See item 4 on the reverse for another way to make an offer to your creditor.)*

3. You can ask for an EXEMPTION. An exemption will protect more, or maybe even all of your earnings. You can get an exemption if you need your earnings to support yourself or your family, ***but you cannot get an exemption if***

   a. You use some of your earnings for luxuries and they aren't really necessary for support; ***OR***
   b. The money you owe is for food, clothing, medical care, or housing; ***OR***
   c. You owe the debt for past due child support or spousal support (alimony); ***OR***
   d. You owe the debt to a former employee for wages.

HOW DO YOU ASK FOR AN EXEMPTION?

(See the reverse of this form for instructions about claiming an exemption.)

(Continued on reverse)

HOW DO YOU ASK FOR AN EXEMPTION?

1. Call or write the levying officer for three (3) copies each of the forms called "Claim of Exemption" and "Financial Statement." These forms are free. The name and address of the levying officer are in the big box on the right at the top of the **EWO**.
2. Fill out both forms. On the forms are some sentences or words which have boxes ☐ in front of them. The box means the words which follow may not aply to your case. If the words do apply, put a check in the box.
3. Remember, it is ***your*** job to prove with the Financial Statement form that your earnings are needed for support. Write down the details about your needs.

   For example, if your child has special medical expenses, tell which child, what illnesses, who the doctor is, how often the doctor must be visited, the cost per visit, and the costs of medicines. These details should be listed in item 6. If you need more space, put "See attachment 6" and attach a typed 8½ by 11 sheet of paper on which you have explained your expenses in detail.
4. You can use the Claim of Exemption form to make an offer to the judgment creditor to have a specified amount withheld each pay period. Complete item 3 on the form to indicate the amount you agree to have withheld **each pay day during the withholding period.** (Be sure it's less than the amount to be withheld otherwise.) If your creditor accepts your offer, he will not oppose your claim of exemption. (See (1) below.)
5. Sign the Claim of Exemption and Financial Statement forms. Be sure the Claim of Exemption form shows the address where you receive mail.
6. Mail or deliver two (2) copies of each of the two forms to the levying officer. Keep one copy for yourself in case a court hearing is necessary.

Do not use the Claim of Exemption and Financial Statement forms to seek a modification of child support or alimony payments. These payments can be modified only by the family law court that ordered them.

FILE YOUR CLAIM OF EXEMPTION AS SOON AS POSSIBLE FOR THE MOST PROTECTION.

ONE OF TWO THINGS WILL HAPPEN NEXT

(1) The judgment creditor will not *oppose* (object to) your claim of exemption. If this happens, after 10 days the levying officer will tell your employer to stop withholding or withhold less from your earnings. The part (or all) of your earnings needed for support will be paid to you or paid as you direct. And you will get back earnings the levying officer or your employer were holding when you asked for the exemption.

—OR—

(2) The creditor will *oppose* (object to) your claim of exemption. If this happens, you will receive a Notice of Opposition and Notice of Hearing on Claim of Exemption, in which the creditor states why your exemption should not be allowed. A box in the middle of the Notice of Hearing tells you the time and place of the court hearing which will be in about ten days. Be sure to go to the hearing if you can.

If the judgment creditor has checked the box in item 3 on the Notice of Hearing on Claim of Exemption, the creditor will not be in court. If you are willing to have the court make its decision based on your Financial Statement and the creditor's Notice of Opposition, you need not go to the hearing.

The Notice of Opposition to Claim of Exemption will tell you why the creditor thinks your claim should not be allowed. If you go to the hearing, take any bills, paycheck stubs, cancelled checks, or other evidence (including witnesses) that will help you prove your Claim of Exemption and Financial Statement are correct and your earnings are needed to support yourself or your family.

Perhaps you can even prove the Notice of Opposition is wrong. For example, perhaps the Notice of Opposition states that the judgment was for a common necessary of life. This term is generally taken by courts to mean only the essentials that everyone needs to live; sometimes a court will have to decide the matter. For example, while a coat may be a "common necessary," a fur coat may not be.

If the judge at the hearing agrees with you, your employer will be ordered to stop withholding your earnings or withhold less money. The judge can even order that the **EWO** end before the hearing (so you would get some earnings back).

If the judge does *not* agree with you, the withholding will continue unless you **appeal** to a higher court. The rules for appeals are complex so you should see an attorney if you want to appeal.

If you have one court hearing, you should not file another Claim of Exemption about the same **EWO** unless your finances have gotten worse in an important way.

If your **EWO** is to be changed or ended, the levying officer must sign the notice to your employer of the change. He may give you permission to deliver it to the employer, or it can be mailed.

WHAT HAPPENS TO YOUR EARNINGS IF YOU FILE A CLAIM OF EXEMPTION?

Your employer must continue to hold back part of your earnings for the **EWO** until he receives a notice signed by the levying officer to change the order or end it early.

The levying officer will keep your withheld earnings until your Claim of Exemption is denied or takes effect. At that time your earnings will be paid according to the law that applies to your case.

REGARDING CHILD SUPPORT

If you are obligated to make child support payments, the family support division of your district attorney's office may help you to have an Order Assigning Salary or Wages entered. This order has the top priority claim on your earnings. When it is in effect, little or no money may be available to be withheld for an **EWO**. And if the district attorney is involved in collecting this support from you, he may agree to accept less money if this special order is entered.

WHAT IF YOU STILL HAVE QUESTIONS?

If you cannot see an attorney, or don't want to see an attorney, you might be able to answer some of your questions by reading the law in a law library. Ask the law librarian to help you find sections 706.050 and 706.105 of the California Code of Civil Procedure. Other sections of the code, beginning with section 706.010 may also answer some of your questions.

Also, the office of the Wage and Hour Division of the U.S. Department of Labor may be able to answer some of your questions. Offices are listed in the telephone directory under the U.S. Department of Labor in the U.S. Government listing.

INSTRUCCIONES PARA EMPLEADOS

A V I S O

AVISO LEGAL IMPORTANTE PARA EL EMPLEADO
ACERCA DE LAS ORDENES DE RETENCION DE SUELDO

(Embargo de salarios)

La **Orden de Retención de Sueldo** dispone que su patrón pague parte de su sueldo a un oficial de retención de sueldos. Este oficial pagará el dinero retenido al acreedor que haya obtenido una decisión judicial en su contra. La información que sigue puede ayudarle a proteger su sueldo.

NOTICE

IMPORTANT LEGAL NOTICE TO EMPLOYEE
ABOUT EARNINGS WITHHOLDING ORDERS

(Wage Garnishment)

The Earnings Withholding Order requires your employer to pay part of your earnings to the sheriff or other levying officer. The levying officer will pay the money to a creditor who has a court judgment against you. The information below may help you protect the money you earn.

¿PUEDE USTED SER DESPEDIDO POR ESTA RAZON?

No. A usted no lo pueden despedir a menos que sus sueldos hayan sido retenidos antes por una orden judicial diferente. Si se trata solo de la primera vez en que su sueldo será retenido y su patrón lo despide por esta causa, el Comisionado del Trabajo en California (the California Labor Commissioner), que aparece en el directorio telefónico de las ciudades principales, puede ayudarle a que le devuelvan su empleo.

¿QUE CANTIDAD DE SU SUELDO PUEDE SER RETENIDA?

En el reverso de la Orden de Retención de Sueldo (Earnings Witholding Order, que en adelante aparecerá abreviada como **EWO**), que usted reciba, se indican las Instrucciones para el Patrón. Estas explican la cantidad de su sueldo que puede ser retenida. Por lo general, esta cantidad es de cerca del 25% del sueldo que usted lleva a casa durante un período de 90 días, pero puede haber excepciones.

Si usted tiene dificultad en calcular esta cantidad, pídale ayuda a su patrón.

¿HAY ALGO QUE USTED PUEDA HACER?

Sí. Hay varias possibilidades.

(1) Consulte a un abogado. Si usted no conoce a un abogado, averigüe con el Servicio de Consulta de Abogados (Attorney's Referral Service) o con la Oficina de Ayuda Legal (Legal Aid Office) de su condado. (Ambos aparecen en las páginas amarillas del directorio telefónico bajo "Abogados").

Un abogado puede ayudarle a llegar a un acuerdo con su acreedor, o puede ayudarle a evitar que su sueldo sea retenido. También es posible que lo mejor que usted pueda hacer sea declararse en bancarrota o solicitarle a la corte de bancarrotas que le ayude a pagarle a sus acreedores. Estas posibilidades pueden ayudarle a evitar que le retengan sus sueldos.

Un abogado puede ayudarle a hacer la decisión que más le convenga. Llévele la **EWO** al abogado para que le de el mejor consejo y la ayuda más rápida.

(2) Trate de llegar usted mismo a un acuerdo con su acreedor. Llame al acreedor o al abogado del acreedor que aparece en la **EWO**. Si usted llega a un acuerdo, evitará la retención de sus sueldos o bajará la cantidad de la retención según el acuerdo. (Vea el párrafo 4 al reverso de este aviso en el que se describe otra manera de hacerle una oferta a su acreedor).

(3) Usted puede solicitar una EXENCION. Con una exención podrá proteger más y, quizás, hasta todo su sueldo. Usted puede pedir una exención si necesita su sueldo para su propio mantenimiento o el de su familia, **pero no podrá obtener una exención si:**

(a) Utiliza parte de su sueldo para lujos y esa parte no es realmente necesaria para su mantenimiento; **O**

(b) El dinero que usted debe es por alimentos, ropa, tratamiento médico o gastos de vivienda; **O**

(c) Su deuda es por gastos atrasados para el mantenimiento de sus hijos o de su ex-esposa/o (alimentación); **O**

(d) Su deuda es por sueldos que no ha pagado a sus ex-empleados.

VEA EL REVERSO DE ESTE AVISO PARA ENCONTRAR INSTRUCCIONES ACERCA DE COMO HACER UN RECLAMO DE EXENCION

(Continúa al reverso)

COMO SOLICITAR UNA EXENCION

1. Llame o escriba al oficial de retención para pedirle tres copias del formulario llamado "Reclamo de Exención y Declaración Financiera" (Claim of Exemption and Financial Declaration). Estos formularios son gratis. El nombre y la dirección del oficial de retención aparecen en la casilla grande al lado derecho de la parte superior de la **EWO.**

2. Llene el formulario. El formulario tiene frases o palabras que van precedidas por casillas ☐. La casilla significa que las palabras que siguen posiblemente no correspondan a su caso. Si las palabras sí le corresponden, haga una marca en la casilla.

3. Recuerde que, comprobar con este formulario que sus sueldos son necesarios para mantenimiento, es **su** responsabilidad. Ponga por escrito el detalle de sus necesidades.

   Por ejemplo, si su niño tiene gastos médicos especiales, diga cuál niño es, cuáles enfermedades son, quién es el doctor, con qué frecuencia tiene que ver al doctor, el costo de cada visita y el costo de las medicinas. Estos detalles deben aparecer en una lista en el punto 11. Si necesita más espacio escriba en inglés "See attachment 11," (Véase el anexo 11), y añada una hoja 8½ x 11 escrita a máquina, en la cual explicará sus gastos en detalle.

4. Usted peude utilizar el formulario de Reclamo de Exención para hacerle una oferta al acreedor que obtuvo el juicio de manera que solo le retengan una cantidad especificada en cada período de pago. Llene el punto 3 del formulario para indicar la cantidad que usted está de acuerdo que sea retenida. (Asegúrese de que sea **menor** que la cantidad que de otra manera le sería retenida). Si el acreedor acepta su oferta, no se opondrá a su reclamo de exención. (Vea el párrafo (1) más adelante).

5. Firme el formulario al terminar y **asegúrese** de poner la fecha y el lugar donde lo ha firmado. Asegúrese también de indicar en el formulario la dirección donde usted recibe su correo.

6. Envíe por correo o entregue dos copias del formulario al oficial de retención. Guarde una copia en caso de que sea necesaria para una audiencia en la corte.

   No utilice el formulario de Reclamo de Exención para solicitar una modificación de pagos de mantenimiento de sus hijos o de su ex-esposa/o (Alimentación).

PARA OBTENER LA MAYOR PROTECCION, ENVIE SU RECLAMO DE EXENCION LO MAS PRONTO POSIBLE

A CONTINUACION, OCURRIRA UNA DE DOS COSAS

1) El acreedor que obtuvo el juicio no se opondrá (no objetará) a su reclamo de exención. Si ocurre esto, el oficial de retención le informará a su patrón después de 10 días, que descontinúe la retención de sueldos o que retenga una cantidad menor de su sueldo. La parte (o todo) el sueldo que usted necesita para el mantenimiento se le pagará a usted o se pagará como usted ordene. Además, se le devolverán los sueldos que el oficial de retención o su patrón habían retenido cuando usted solicitó la exención.

-o-

2) El acreedor se opondrá (objetará) a su reclamo de exención. Si esto ocurre, usted recibirá un Aviso de Oposición y Aviso de Audiencia sobre Reclamo de Exención (Notice of Opposition and Notice of Hearing and Claim of Exemption), en la cual el acreedor declara por qué su exención no debe de ser aprobada. En el medio del Aviso de Audiencia hay una casilla en la que se le informará sobre la hora y el lugar de la audiencia en la corte, la cual tendrá lugar en aproximadamente diez días. No deje de asistir a la audiencia si puede.

   Si el acreedor que obtuvo el juicio ha marcado la casilla en el punto 3 del Aviso de Oposición y Aviso de Audiencia sobre Reclamo de Exención, el acreedor no comparecerá ante la corte. Si usted está dispuesto a que la corte haga su decisión basándose solamente en su Declaración Financiera y en el Aviso de Oposición del Acreedor, usted no necesitará estar presente en la audiencia.

El Aviso de Oposición al Reclamo de Exención le informará por qué el acreedor opina que su reclamo no debe ser aprobado. Si asiste a la audiencia lleve cualquier cuenta, los comprobantes o talonarios de sus cheques de pago, sus cheques cancelados u otra evidencia (incluyendo testigos) que le ayuden a comprobar que su Reclamo de Exención y Declaración Financiera son correctos y que sus sueldos son necesarios para su mantenimiento o el de su familia.

Quizás hasta pueda comprobar que el Aviso de Oposición esté equivocado. Por ejemplo, quizás el Aviso de Oposición dice que la decisión judicial se hizo por gastos necesarios comunes de subsistencia. Esta expresión generalmente la interpretan las cortes como lo que cada uno necesita especialmente para vivir; a veces la corte tiene que tomar una decisión sobre el asunto. Por ejemplo, aunque un abrigo pueda considerarse como "una necesidad común de subsistencia", un abrigo de pieles finas puede que no lo sea.

Si en la audiencia el juez está de acuerdo con usted, le puede ordenar a su patrón que deje de retenerle su sueldo o que retenga menos dinero. El juez hasta puede ordenar que la **EOW** termine antes de la audiencia (de modo que a usted le devuelvan algunos sueldos ya retenidos).

Si el juez no está de acuerdo con usted, la orden de retención continuará a menos que usted haga una **apelación** ante una corte de mayor autoridad. El procedimiento de apelación es muy complicado así que usted debe de consultar con un abogado si desea apelar.

Si usted ha tenido una audiencia en la corte, no debe de hacer otro Reclamo de Exención sobre la misma **EWO** a menos que sus finanzas hayan empeorado considerablemente.

Si su **EWO** va a ser cambiada o cancelada, el oficial de retención debe firmar el aviso que se le envía a su patrón sobre el cambio. El oficial puede autorizarlo a usted para que se lo entregue a su patrón, o puede enviarlo por correo.

¿QUE OCURRE CON SU SUELDO SI USTED HACE UN RECLAMO DE EXENCION?

Su patrón tiene que continuar reteniendo parte de su sueldo según la **EWO** hasta que reciba un aviso firmado por el oficial de retención para cambiar la orden o cancelarla antes de la fecha indicada.

El oficial de retención se quedará con sus sueldos retenidos hasta que su reclamo de exención sea negado o se ponga en efecto. En ese momento, se le pagarán sus sueldos de acuerdo con la ley que corresponda a sus caso.

SOBRE EL MANTENIMIENTO DE HIJOS

Si usted tiene la obligación de hacer pagos por el mantenimiento de sus niños, la división de mantenimiento familiar de la oficina del fiscal en su condado puede ayudarlo a registrar la Orden de Asignación de Sueldos o Salarios (Order Assigning Salary or Wages). Esta orden tiene prioridad máxima sobre sus sueldos. Cuando se encuentra en vigencia, poco o nada de su dinero estará disponible para que sea retenido por una **EWO**, pero si el fiscal está ya colectando dinero de mantenimiento, el fiscal puede convenir en aceptar menos dinero.

¿QUE PUEDE HACER SI TODAVIA TIENE PREGUNTAS?

Si usted no puede o no quiere consultar con un abogado, es posible que encuentre respuesta a algunas de sus preguntas leyendo la ley en una biblioteca legal. Pídale a la bibliotecaria legal que le ayude a encontrar las secciones 723.050 y 723.105 del Código de Procedimiento Civil de California (California Code of Civil Procedure). Otras secciones del Código, comenzando con la sección 723.010, pueden también contestar algunas de sus preguntas.

Además, puede ser que la Oficina de Salario y División de Horas del Departamento de Trabajo de los Estados Unidos (Wage and Hour Division of the U.S. Department of Labor) pueda contestarle algunas de sus preguntas. Estas oficinas aparecen en el directorio telefónico bajo el encabezamiento "Departmento de Trabajo de los Estados Unidos" en la sección de oficinas del Gobierno de los Estados Unidos (U.S. Department of Labor, U.S. Government listings).

Employer's Duties After Being Served With Earnings Withholding Order

[§7.73] Duration of Withholding Period; Payment to Levying Officer

The 100th day after service of the earnings withholding order on the employer is no longer used in determining the end of the withholding period. CCP §706.022(a). The date of termination of a dormant or suspended earnings withholding order under CCP §706.032 is now included in the list of dates on which the withholding period terminates. CCP §706.022(a)(4). The other definitions of "withholding period," discussed in Book §7.73, remain in effect.

Under CCP §706.024, the amount required to satisfy the order is the total amount required to satisfy the writ of execution on the date the order is issued, with the following additions and subtractions:

(1) The addition of the statutory fee for service of the order and any other statutory fees for performing duties under the order.

(2) The addition of costs added to the order under CCP §685.090.

(3) The subtraction of the amount of any partial satisfactions.

(4) The addition of daily interest accruing after issuance of the order, as adjusted for partial satisfactions.

At least once every two years, the levying officer must file an account with the court for all amounts collected under the earnings withholding order, including costs and interest added to the amount due. CCP §706.026(b).

If withholding under an earnings withholding order stops because the judgment debtor's employment has terminated, the earnings withholding order terminates at the end of a continuous 180-day period during which no amounts are withheld under the order. CCP §706.032(a)(1). If withholding under the withholding order stops because the judgment debtor's earnings are subject to an order or assignment with higher priority, the earnings withholding order terminates at the end of a continuous two-year period during which no amounts are withheld under the order. CCP §706.032(a)(2). If an earnings withholding order has terminated under CCP §706.032(a), the employer must return the order to the levying officer along with a statement of the reasons for returning the order. CCP §706.032(b).

If the writ is returned before the earnings withholding order terminates, the levying officer, on termination of the order, must make a supplemental return on the writ. The supplemental return must contain the same information as an original return under CCP §699.560. CCP §706.033.

Priority

[§7.75] When Wage Assignment for Support Involved

Wages withheld pursuant to a wage assignment for spousal support are not exempt from levy under a writ of execution to enforce a money judgment against the supported spouse. *Vineyard v Sisson* (1990) 223 CA3d 931, 272 CR 914. However, an employer, simultaneously bound by a wage assignment order for spousal support and a writ of execution against the supported spouse's interest in the supporting spouse's wages, must pay to the supported spouse all the supporting spouse's wages subject to the assignment, unless the judgment creditor has obtained a court order altering the statutory priority. 223 CA3d at 939.

Effective January 1, 1994, CCP §706.031 substituted the term "earnings assignment order for support" for the term "wage assignment for support."

An employer who willfully fails to withhold and forward support pursuant to a currently valid assignment order entered and served on the employer is liable for the amount of support not withheld, forwarded, or otherwise paid to the obligee. Fam C §5241(a). In addition, an employer's willful failure to comply with an assignment order is punishable as contempt under CCP §1218. Fam C §5241(b).

Earnings Exempt From Withholding

State Exemption

[§7.81] Earnings Withholding Order for Support

Effective January 1, 1994, CCP §706.052(a) substituted the term "earnings assignment order for support" for "wage assignment for support." An earnings assignment order for support is an order made under Fam C §§5200–5295 or Prob C §3088 that requires an employer to withhold earnings for support. CCP §706.011(b).

Service of Subsequent Earnings Withholding Order by Same Judgment Creditor

[§7.82] Time Limitation

Former CCP §706.107 has been repealed and replaced by CCP §706.023. Unless otherwise provided in the statutory scheme, CCP §706.023(a) requires that an employer comply with the first earnings withholding order served on the employer. If the employer is served with more than one order on the same day, the employer must comply with the order issued under the judgment that was entered first. If orders served on the same day are based on judgments entered on the same day, the employer is free to choose which of these orders require compliance. CCP §706.023(b). If an earnings withholding order is served while the employer is required to comply with another earnings withholding order regarding the same employee, the later order is ineffective and the employer may not withhold earnings under the later order. CCP §706.023(c).

[§7.83] For Recovery of Costs and Interest

Former CCP §706.028 has been repealed and replaced by a new version of §706.028, which is substantially similar in content to its predecessor. Under §706.028, however, the additional earnings withholding order is designated "final earnings withholding order for costs and interest." This order is issued only after an earlier earnings withholding order has been returned satisfied. CCP §706.028(a). In addition, CCP §706.028(c) explicitly states that a final withholding order for costs and interest must be enforced in the same manner as other earnings withholding orders. Note also that interest stops accruing on the date the final withholding order is issued. Other costs may not be added after that date, except for the statutory fee for service of the order and any other statutory fees for performing duties under the order. CCP §706.028(d).

Former CCP §706.107 has been repealed and replaced by CCP §706.023. For further discussion, see Update §7.82.

8

Examination and Other Proceedings

PRACTICAL CONSIDERATIONS

[§8.4] When Service on Judgment Creditor's or Judgment Debtor's Attorney Is Proper

Effective January 1, 1994, former CC §4809 was repealed and replaced by Fam C §215, which is substantially the same.

EXAMINATION PROCEEDINGS

Initiating Procedure Against Judgment Debtor

[§8.7] Service of Order; Lien

In *In re Hilde* (Zimmerman v Southern Cal. Bank) (9th Cir 1997) 120 F3d 950, the Ninth Circuit held that service of the order to appear for an examination creates a lien and that no further steps to perfect the lien are required.

The Examination

[§8.19] Counseling Debtor

For a case discussing the debtor's right to claim exemptions following issuance of a turnover order under CCP §708.205 for assets disclosed at a debtor's examination, see *Imperial Bank v Pim Elec., Inc.* (1995) 33 CA4th 540, 39 CR2d 432. See also *In re Hilde* (Zimmerman v Southern Cal. Bank) (9th Cir 1997) 120 F3d 950, which holds that service of an order to appear for examination pursuant to CCP §708.110 creates a lien and the lien thus created has priority over the claim of a bankruptcy trustee in a bankruptcy proceeding filed more than 90 days after the lien is created. The Ninth Circuit specifically rejected the contention that *Imperial Bank* stands for the proposition that a turnover order is necessary to perfect the lien created by service of an order to appear for examination pursuant to CCP §708.110(d).

[§8.22] Witnesses; Privileges

Although CCP §708.130 permits examination "in the same manner as upon the trial of an issue," and Evid C §§1152 and 1154 generally preclude any trial examination regarding a party's settlement discussions, questions regarding settlement discussions are nonetheless permissible in a debtor's examination. *Young v Keele* (1987) 188 CA3d 1090, 233 CR 850. Evidence Code §§1152 and 1154 are intended to encourage settlement before trial, which is irrelevant to an examination after judgment when the creditor is seeking to elicit full disclosure of the debtor's assets.

[§8.23] Sample Questionnaire for Judgment Debtor

The exemption amount for the loan value of unmatured life insurance policies under CCP §740.100(b) has been increased to $8000.

Determination When Third Person Claims Interest in Property or Denies Debt

[§8.27] Determination by Court

For a recent case applying CCP §708.180, see *Evans v Paye* (1995) 32 CA4th 265, 37 CR2d 915, in which the appellate court upheld the trial court's finding that a son's denial of the existence of a debt owed to his father, the judgment debtor, was not made in good faith.

Failure To Appear

Contempt

[§8.31] Procedure in General

Former CCP §904.1(a)(2) has been redesignated CCP §904.1(a)(1).

Code of Civil Procedure §1218 has been amended to provide that the court may award attorney fees and costs to a party initiating a contempt proceeding against a person subject to a court order as a party to the action adjudged guilty of contempt for violating that court order.

2 California Civil Procedure During Trial §§14.50–14.58 (Cal CEB 1984) have been replaced by 2 California Trial Practice: Civil Procedure During Trial §§16.99–16.129 (3d ed Cal CEB 1995).

[§8.34] WRITTEN INTERROGATORIES TO JUDGMENT DEBTOR

The availability of sanctions for failure to answer interrogatories is now governed by CCP §2030(k). Section 2030(k) does not specifically authorize the court to punish a party's failure to answer interrogatories as a contempt. Nonetheless, the statute authorizes the court to "make those orders that are just."

The 35-interrogatory limit under CCP §2030 applies to each set of interrogatories propounded under CCP §708.020 but "does not apply cumulatively to interrogatories propounded by a judgment creditor to a judgment debtor." CCP §708.020(d).

The judgment creditor may not serve interrogatories under CCP §708.020 within 120 days after the judgment debtor has responded to interrogatories or demands for inspection previously served under CCP §708.020 or §708.030, or within 120 days after the judgment debtor has been examined under CCP §§708.110–708.205. The judgment debtor is not required to respond to any discovery so served. CCP §708.030(b).

For discussion of a demand for inspection of documents in aid of enforcing a judgment, see Update §8.34A.

For a comprehensive discussion of discovery procedures, see Civil Discovery Practice in California (Cal CEB 1988).

[§8.34A] DEMAND FOR INSPECTION OF DOCUMENTS

The judgment creditor may now make a demand for production and inspection of documents in the judgment debtor's possession, custody, or control, if the demand requests information to aid in enforcement of the money judgment. The demand and response must comply with the requirements of CCP §2031. CCP §708.030(a). On the requirements of CCP §2031, see 2 Civil Discovery Practice in California §§9.19–9.28 (Cal CEB 1988).

The judgment creditor may not serve a demand for inspection under CCP §708.030 within 120 days after the judgment debtor has responded to interrogatories or demands for inspection previously served under CCP §708.020 or §708.030, or within 120 days after the judgment debtor has been examined under CCP §§708.110–708.205. The judgment debtor is not required to respond to any discovery so served. CCP §708.030(b).

Inspection demands served under CCP §708.030 may be enforced to the extent practicable, in the same manner as inspection demands in a civil action. CCP §708.030(c). On enforcement of inspection demands in a civil action, see 2 Civil Discovery Practice in California §§9.33–9.36 (Cal CEB 1988).

CREDITORS' SUITS

[§8.35] Nature of Proceedings

A creditor's suit is an equitable action, independent of the action in which the judgment was obtained. Thus, in making its determination in a creditor's suit, the court is not limited to the four corners of the previous judgment. It must consider whether the circumstances surrounding the entry of the prior judgment render inequitable its enforcement by lien. *Fansler v Fansler* (1988) 206 CA3d 81, 253 CR 186, relying on *Holstein v Superior Court* (1969) 275 CA2d 708, 80 CR 301, and *Woodcock v*

The Petrol Corp. (1941) 48 CA2d 652, 120 P2d 889. The court in *Fansler* also held that motions to impose liens on third party obligations and to determine the priority of competing liens are subject to the same principles of equity that govern creditors' suits.

LIEN IN PENDING ACTION OR PROCEEDING

[§8.48] Judgment Creditor's Intervention in Pending Action or Proceeding

For a case applying CCP §708.430, allowing a judgment creditor to intervene in an action in which the judgment debtor might be entitled to money or property, see *Marriage of Kerr* (1986) 185 CA3d 130, 229 CR 610.

Enforcement of Lien

[§8.51] Under Court Order

A division of community property in a marital dissolution proceeding may constitute a transfer of property under CCP §708.470(c). *Marriage of Katz* (1991) 234 CA3d 1711, 286 CR 495 (transfer to spouse in course of marital dissolution proceeding of more than one half of undivided community property interest supported liability to creditor under CCP §708.470(c)).

ASSIGNMENT ORDERS

[§8.58] Priority of Assignments

Notwithstanding CC §§955 and 955.1, the assignee of a nonnegotiable instrument takes the instrument subject to all defenses and equities existing in favor of the obligor before notice of the assignment. *Royal Bank Export Fin. Co. v Bestways Distrib. Co.* (1991) 229 CA3d 764, 280 CR 355. Civil Code §§955 and 955.1 only control the effect and priority of the assignment order.

Obligor's Rights

[§8.60] Form: Notice of Assignment Order

The title of the form printed in Book §8.60 is incorrect. The proper title is "Notice of Assignment Order."

[§8.75] ENFORCEMENT AFTER DEATH OF JUDGMENT CREDITOR OR JUDGMENT DEBTOR

Code of Civil Procedure §686.020 has been amended to state that after the death of the judgment debtor, enforcement of a judgment against property in the judgment debtor's estate is governed by the Probate Code.

See Prob C §§9300–9304. See also 3 California Decedent Estate Practice §§33.35–33.39 (Cal CEB 1987).

If the creditor takes out a life insurance policy on the debtor and names itself as beneficiary, on the debtor's death, the creditor may not collect more than the amount of the debt, plus the premiums paid on the policy, and the interest on both those amounts. *Jimenez v Protective Life Ins. Co.* (1992) 8 CA4th 528, 540, 10 CR2d 326, 333. In *Jimenez,* the court reasoned that the creditor/beneficiary could not recover in excess of its insurable interest under the policy.

INTERESTS AND COSTS

[§8.76] Interest

The 10-percent interest rate provided in CCP §685.010(a) does not apply to judgments against local public entities under Govt C §970.1(b). The 7-percent interest rate specified in Cal Const art XV, §1 applies instead. *California Fed Sav. & Loan Ass'n v City of Los Angeles* (1995) 11 C4th 342, 45 CR2d 279; *San Francisco Unified School Dist. v San Francisco Classroom Teachers Ass'n* (1990) 222 CA3d 146, 272 CR 38. Code of Civil Procedure §685.030(a) provides that if a money judgment is satisfied in full under a writ issued under the Enforcement of Judgments Law (CCP §§680.010–724.260), interest ceases to accrue on the judgment on the date of levy if the proceeds are paid in a lump sum, ceases on the date and in the manner provided in CCP §706.024 or §706.028 if the judgment is satisfied pursuant to an earnings withholding order and, in any other case, ceases on the date the proceeds of sale or collection are actually received by the levying officer.

Former CCP §685.030(a)(2) has been redesignated CCP §685.030(a)(3).

Code of Civil Procedure §685.030(e) has been added to state that:

> The clerk of a municipal or justice court may enter in the Register of Actions a writ of execution on a money judgment as returned wholly satisfied when the judgment amount, as specified on the writ, is fully collected and only an interest deficit of no more than ten dollars ($10) exists, due to automation of the continual daily interest accrual calculation.

Costs

[§8.77] Recoverable Costs Generally

Attorney fees incurred in enforcing a judgment may be claimed as costs if the underlying judgment includes an award of attorney fees based on a contract between the judgment creditor and the judgment debtor. CCP §§685.040, 685.070(a)(6), 1033.5(a)(10)(A).

Claiming Costs Allowable Under CCP §685.070

[§8.78] Specific Costs Allowed

Attorney fees incurred in enforcing a judgment may be claimed as costs if the underlying judgment includes an award of attorney fees based on a contract between the judgment creditor and the judgment debtor. CCP §§685.040, 685.070(a)(6), 1033.5(a)(10)(A).

Procedure

[§8.79] Memorandum of Costs; Time Limitation

If a memorandum of costs for the statutory costs specified in CCP §685.070(a) is filed with an application for a writ of execution, those costs not already allowed by the court may be included in the amount specified in the writ of execution (in a total amount not greater than $100), subject to a later disallowance as ordered by the court under a motion to tax. The memorandum of costs must contain the following statement: "The fees sought under this memorandum may be disallowed by a court upon a motion to tax filed by the debtor notwithstanding the fees having been included in the writ of execution." CCP §685.070(e).

Effective January 1, 1997, CCP §685.070(f) provides that CCP §1013, extending the time within which a right may be exercised or an act may be done, applies to the time period specified in CCP §685.070.

Motion To Recover Costs

[§8.83] Form: Notice of Motion for Order Fixing Costs of Enforcement of Judgment (CCP §685.080)

Comment: Former CC §4809 was repealed effective January 1, 1994. It has been replaced by Fam C §215, which is substantially the same.

[§8.86] Adding Recovered Costs to Principal Amount of Judgment Remaining Unsatisfied

The costs of an outstanding earnings withholding order are now treated the same as an outstanding writ. CCP §685.090(c).

9

Exemptions; Homesteads

EXEMPTIONS FROM LEVY OF EXECUTION

[§9.6] Judicial Council Checklist: Types of Exempt Property

In *Mackey v Lanier Collections Agency & Serv., Inc.* (1988) 486 US 825, 100 L Ed 2d 836, 108 S Ct 2182, the Supreme Court held that the Employee Retirement Income Security Act of 1974 (ERISA) (29 USC

§§1001–1461) preempted a Georgia statute that exempted from garnishment funds from an ERISA-qualified employee benefit plan. Even though ERISA bars garnishment of employee *pension* benefits, there is no such protection for employee *welfare* benefits. Thus, the Court allowed garnishment of such benefits despite the state statute prohibiting levy on them. ERISA should be examined to ascertain whether it allows execution in spite of CCP §704.115 provisions that may disallow it.

In *In re MacIntyre* (De Massa v MacIntyre) (9th Cir 1996) 74 F3d 186, the Ninth Circuit held that IRC §403(b) plan annuities were fully exempt under CCP §704.115(a)(1) as "private retirement plans." See also *In re Cheng* (Cheng v Gill) (9th Cir 1991) 943 F2d 1114 (sole shareholder's corporate retirement plan held fully exempt).

Government Code §31452 exempts from execution property purchased for investment purposes under the County Employees Retirement Law of 1937 (Govt C §§31450–31895). In *Parsons Brinckerhoff Quade & Douglas, Inc. v Kern County Employees Retirement Ass'n* (1992) 5 CA4th 1264, 7 CR2d 456, the court held that Govt C §31452 is unconstitutional when applied to the enforcement of a mechanics' lien by a claimant whose lien rights are guaranteed by Cal Const art XIV, §3.

Particular Property and Situations

[§9.19] Motor Vehicles

The exempt equity amount for motor vehicles under CCP §704.010 has been increased to $1900.

[§9.20] Tools; Property Used To Earn Livelihood

The exempt equity amount for tools or other personal property used by the debtor to earn a livelihood under CCP §704.060 has been increased to $5000.

Jointly Owned Property

[§9.23] Partnership Property

Two fairly recent cases have dealt with the conditions that must be satisfied before a court may authorize the foreclosure and sale of a debtor partner's partnership *interest,* as distinct from partnership assets. In *Crocker Nat'l Bank v Perroton* (1989) 208 CA3d 1, 255 CR 794, the court of appeal specified three conditions that must be met to reach the partnership interest: (1) the creditor has obtained a charging order, (2) the judgment remains unsatisfied, and (3) all partners other than the debtor have consented to the sale of the interest. In *Hellman v Anderson* (1991) 233 CA3d 840, 284 CR 830, the court generally agreed with *Perroton* except the court held that the consent of nondebtor partners to the sale is not an essential condition, provided the foreclosure does not unduly interfere with partnership business. The effect of foreclosure on the partnership must be evaluated on a case-by-case basis by the trial court in connection with its equitable power of foreclosure. 233 CA3d at 851. The court in *Hellman* placed on the partner debtor the burden of proving the effect of foreclosure on the partnership. 233 CA3d at 853. Like the court in *Perroton, Hellman* emphasized that foreclosure and sale is only permissible on a partner's "interest in the partnership," meaning only the partner's share of profits and surplus. A partner's interest subject to foreclosure and sale does not include the partner's right in specific partnership property nor the right to participate in management. 233 CA3d at 846.

Effective June 6, 1996, CCP §699.720(a)(2) was amended to include interests in a limited liability company in the category of types of property not subject to execution.

Bankruptcy

[§9.26] General Procedure

Federal Rules of Bankruptcy Procedure 4003(b) provides that objections to the debtor's list of property claimed as exempt must be filed within 30 days after the conclusion of the meeting of creditors held pursuant to Rule 2003(a) or the filing of any amendment to the list or supplemental schedules filed under Fed R Bankr P 1007(h) unless, within that period, further time is granted by the court.

For further discussion of exemptions in bankruptcy cases, see Update §§10.20–10.22.

[§9.27] Electing Alternative State Exemptions

The debtor's choice of exemptions will affect the debtor's ability to exempt certain assets. For example, if the debtor selects the exemptions available under CCP §703.140, California's counterpart to the federal exemptions, the debtor's IRA will not be exempt. See *In re Innis* (Bankr SD Cal 1986) 62 BR 659. On the other hand, if the debtor elects the California exemptions, the IRA will be exempt. See *In re Vigghiany* (Bankr SD Cal 1987) 74 BR 61.

Married debtors may only claim one set of exemptions. CCP §703.110. This prohibition of exemption stacking was upheld as constitutional in *In re Talmadge* (9th Cir 1987) 832 F2d 1120.

All the exemptions under CCP §§703.010–704.995 are available to the debtor, regardless of whether there is a money judgment against the debtor or a money judgment is being enforced by execution sale or other procedure. *In re Pladson* (Kendall v Pladson) (9th Cir 1994) 35 F3d 462.

[§9.27A] Retirement Plans

Code of Civil Procedure §704.115 enables a debtor to exempt (1) private retirement plans, (2) profit-sharing plans designed and used for retirement purposes, and (3) self-employed retirement plans and individual retirement accounts to the extent the amounts held do not exceed the amounts exempt from federal income tax. Self-employed retirement plans and individual retirement accounts are exempt only to the extent necessary to provide for the support of the judgment debtor in retirement. CCP §704.115(e). See *In re Rawlinson* (Rawlinson v Kendall) (Bankr 9th Cir 1997) 209 BR 501, in which the Ninth Circuit Bankruptcy Appellate Panel held that an individual retirement account could be claimed as exempt under CCP §703.140(b)(10)(E) (as a "similar plan or contract"). See also *In re MacIntyre* (De Massa v MacIntyre) (9th Cir 1996) 74 F3d 186; *In re Cheng* (Cheng v Gill) (9th Cir 1991) 943 F2d 1114.

A debtor does not forfeit this exemption by borrowing extensively from the plan. See *In re Bloom* (9th Cir 1988) 839 F2d 1376.

An ERISA-qualified pension plan is not the property of the debtor's bankruptcy estate under 11 USC §541(c)(2). *Patterson v Shumate* (1992) 504 US 753, 119 L Ed 2d 519, 112 S Ct 2242. Settling a long-standing dispute, the United States Supreme Court reasoned that the phrase "applicable nonbankruptcy law" in 11 USC §541(c)(2) included the antialienation and antiassignment provisions of the Employee Retirement Income Security Act of 1974 (ERISA) (29 USC §§1001–1461).

[§9.31] Exemptions in Federal Statutes

The reference to 38 USC §3101(a) in the Book is an error. The exemption from attachment or execution for veterans' disability benefits is found at 38 USC §5301(a).

A state law may authorize seizure of veterans' disability payments to satisfy child support obligations. Such a law is consistent with both federal law and congressional intent that a veteran's disability payments be used to support the veteran as well as the veteran's family. *Rose v Rose* (1987) 481 US 619, 95 L Ed 2d 599, 107 S Ct 2029.

EXEMPTION FROM WAGE GARNISHMENT

Procedure

Opposing Claim

[§9.42] Judicial Council Form 982.5(6): Notice of Filing of Claim of Exemption

ATTORNEY OR PARTY WITHOUT ATTORNEY *(Name and Address)*: TELEPHONE NO.: ATTORNEY FOR *(Name)*:	LEVYING OFFICER *(Name and Address)*:
NAME OF COURT, JUDICIAL DISTRICT, AND BRANCH COURT, IF ANY:	
PLAINTIFF: DEFENDANT:	
NOTICE OF FILING OF CLAIM OF EXEMPTION **(Wage Garnishment)**	LEVYING OFFICER FILE NUMBER:
	COURT CASE NUMBER:

TO THE JUDGMENT CREDITOR:

Name and address

1. This notice was mailed on *(date)*: at *(place)*: , California.

2. The judgment debtor (employee) has filed the attached Claim of Exemption form and Financial Statement form. The Earnings Withholding Order will be changed as requested by the debtor in item 3 of the Claim of Exemption ***unless you oppose the Claim of Exemption.*** To oppose the Claim of Exemption, you must schedule a court hearing and follow the procedures described below.

Levying Officer, by

(TYPE OR PRINT NAME) *(SIGNATURE)*

— INSTRUCTIONS TO JUDGMENT CREDITOR —

3. You must complete all of the following steps **within 10 days of the mailing date shown above in item 1:**

HOW DO I OPPOSE THE CLAIM OF EXEMPTION?

a. Obtain at least five copies each of the following printed forms:
   (1) Notice of Opposition to Claim of Exemption, and
   (2) Notice of Hearing on Claim of Exemption.
   These forms are available from the clerk of the court.

b. Contact the clerk of the court about setting a hearing date, time, and place. The date of the **hearing must be not more than 30 days after the date you file your paper with the court.** You must file your paper with the court within 10 days of the date shown in item 1.

c. Complete all five copies of both forms.

(Continued on reverse)

PLAINTIFF:	LEVYING OFFICER FILE NO.:	COURT CASE NUMBER:
DEFENDANT:		

INSTRUCTIONS TO JUDGMENT CREDITOR (continued)

3. *(Continued)*

WHAT DO I FILE WITH THE LEVYING OFFICER?

d. Give the following documents to the LEVYING OFFICER whose name and address are on the front of this form:
   (1) the **original** Notice of Opposition to Claim of Exemption with **original** signature, and
   (2) a copy of Notice of Hearing on Claim of Exemption.
   The levying officer must receive the Notice of Opposition to Claim of Exemption within 10 days of the mailing date in item 1 on the front of this form, or the Earnings Withholding Order will be released or changed as requested in the Claim of Exemption.

WHAT DO I FILE WITH THE COURT?

e. File the following document with the COURT:
   – the **original** Notice of Hearing on Claim of Exemption with **original** signature.
   Make sure that the Proof of Service on the reverse has been completed as indicated in paragraph 3g below and that the necessary signature on the Proof of Service is original.
   The court must receive this document within 10 days of the mailing date shown in item 1 on the front of this form.
   Before the hearing, **the levying officer** will file the original Claim of Exemption and the original Notice of Opposition to Claim of Exemption with the court.

WHAT DO I SERVE ON THE JUDGMENT DEBTOR?

f. Have one copy each of the
   (1) Notice of Opposition to Claim of Exemption, and
   (2) Notice of Hearing on Claim of Exemption
   served on the judgment debtor (employee) or the debtor's attorney at the address shown in item 2 on the Claim of Exemption. They must be served 15 days before the hearing if they are personally served. If they are mailed to an address within California, they must be mailed 20 days before the hearing. If they are mailed to an address outside California, they must be mailed 25 days before the hearing.
   Complete the Proof of Service as shown in item 3g below.

g. Service of the Notice of Opposition to Claim of Exemption and Notice of Hearing on Claim of Exemption must be made by first class mail or personal delivery. Service must be made by someone **not** a party to the action (not the judgment creditor). After the notices are served, the person making the service must complete and sign the appropriate Proof of Service on the reverse of the signed **original** Notice of Hearing on Claim of Exemption which will be filed with the court.

4. Take a copy of each form and the Claim of Exemption with you to the court hearing.

   If you will not attend the court hearing, **check item 3 on the Notice of Hearing on Claim of Exemption.**

HOMESTEADS

[§9.48] General Principles

Code of Civil Procedure §704.730(a)(2) has been amended to increase the homestead exemption to $75,000 if the judgment debtor or spouse of the judgment debtor who resides in the homestead is at the time of the attempted sale a member of a family unit, and there is at least one member of the family unit who owns no interest in the homestead or whose only interest in the homestead is a community property interest with the judgment debtor.

Code of Civil Procedure §704.730(a)(3) has been amended to increase the homestead exemption to $100,000 if the judgment debtor or spouse of the judgment debtor who resides at the homestead is, at the time of the homestead's attempted sale, either 65 years of age or older, or physically or mentally disabled. In addition, this exemption has been extended to persons 55 years of age or older with a gross annual income of not more than $15,000 or, if the judgment debtor is married, a gross annual income, including the gross annual income of the judgment debtor's spouse, of not more than $20,000 and the sale is an involuntary sale.

Code of Civil Procedure §704.730(a)(1) has been amended to increase the homestead exemption to $50,000 unless the judgment debtor or spouse of the judgment debtor who resides in the homestead is a person described in CCP §704.730(a)(2) or (3).

The amount of the homestead exemption is determined at the time that a judgment lien is obtained, not at the time the levy of execution is made on the property. CCP §703.050(a); *Berhanu v Metzger* (1992) 12 CA4th 445, 15 CR2d 191.

Declared Homestead

[§9.49] Definition

A declared homestead exemption does not require actual or continuous residence in the homestead. *Webb v Trippet* (1991) 235 CA3d 647, 286 CR 742. However, in an effort to balance the competing interests of debtor and creditor, the court in *Webb* ruled that a declared homestead exemption will be lost after five years if the debtor does not return to inhabit the homestead property within this period of time, or is shown in the meantime to have established another dwelling as his principal residence. 235 CA3d at 652.

Levy Procedure

[§9.57] Hearing

Code of Civil Procedure §704.780(b) has been amended to provide that a court not make an order for sale of a dwelling subject to the homestead exemption if it determines that the sale would not be likely to produce a bid sufficient to satisfy any part of the amount due on the judgment pursuant to CCP §704.800.

10

Debtor and Creditor Bankruptcy Practice: An Overview

[§10.1] INTRODUCTION

On October 22, 1994, President Clinton signed into law the Bankruptcy Reform Act of 1994 (Pub L 103–394, 108 Stat 4106). The 1994 Act made several changes to existing law. Generally speaking, the changes effected by the 1994 Act are applicable to cases filed after October 22, 1994 (Pub L 103–394 §702, 108 Stat 4150), but there are exceptions that apply to specific amended sections of the revised Bankruptcy Code.

The cross-references in the first paragraph of Book §10.1 to §§10.2–10.10 and to §§10.11–10.27 should be to §§10.6–10.33 and 10.34–10.35, respectively.

SUMMARY OF BANKRUPTCY LAW AND PROCEDURE

[§10.2] Bankruptcy Code

Former Chapter 15 of the Bankruptcy Code (former 11 USC §§1501–151326), establishing a pilot program for United States trustees in eight judicial districts, was repealed in 1986. It was replaced by 28 USC §§581–589a, which divide the United States into 21 regions (each region containing one or more judicial districts) and provide for a United States trustee for each region to be appointed by the United States Attorney General. The program is funded by increased filing fees in all cases and quarterly maintenance fees in Chapter 11 cases. 28 USC §589a.

[§10.3] Bankruptcy Rules and Official Forms

The federal bankruptcy rules have been amended several times since their enactment. The rules are now properly cited as the Federal Rules of Bankruptcy Procedure, rather than the Bankruptcy Rules. This citation form parallels the citation form for other federal procedural rules (*e.g.*, the Federal Rules of Civil Procedure).

The official forms, while obligatory in character, are subject to a rule of substantial compliance. Federal Rules of Bankruptcy Procedure 9009 expressly permits the user of the official forms to make such alterations as may be appropriate. The official forms have been revised to make them compatible with electronic systems for docketing and noticing in bankruptcy cases. For example, the format of the petition (Form 1) is now prescribed to ensure that the clerk of the bankruptcy court has all the necessary information for entry into the court's data base at the inception of the case. The petition, schedules (Form 6), and statement of financial affairs (Form 7) are to be prepunched with two holes at the top, with a sufficient top margin so that they may be placed in the court file without destroying or obscuring the caption or text.

[§10.4] Bankruptcy Courts and Judges

The 1994 Act made key revisions to 11 USC §105 dealing with the powers of a bankruptcy court. New 11 USC §105(d)(1) generally authorizes the bankruptcy court to hold status conferences in bankruptcy cases, while new §105(d)(2) specifically authorizes the bankruptcy court to issue orders to ensure that a case is "handled expeditiously and economically." Thus, the court can do such things as set deadlines for the assumption or rejection of executory contracts or unexpired leases or, in Chapter 11 cases, dates for filing a disclosure statement and plan and other dates relating to the plan confirmation process.

On the use of Fed R Bankr P 9011 to impose sanctions, see *In re Rainbow Magazine, Inc.* (Caldwell v United Capital Group) (9th Cir 1996) 77 F3d 278 (sanctions against principal of Chapter 7 debtor who engineered bad faith filing); *In re Tyler* (Commonwealth Mortgage Co. of Am. v Tyler) (Bankr 9th Cir 1992) 147 BR 208. *Rainbow Magazine* also discusses the contempt power of bankruptcy courts under Fed R Bankr P 9020.

The 1994 Act has partially addressed whether bankruptcy courts may conduct jury trials in fraudulent transfer and preference cases. Title 28 USC §157(e) now permits the bankruptcy court to conduct a jury trial if the district court designates that the bankruptcy judge may do so and the parties consent. Absent such designation and consent, however, case law may still be relevant in determining both the right to a jury trial in particular cases and whether the bankruptcy court has inherent power to conduct a jury trial. See *Langenkamp v Culp* (1990) 498 US 42, 112 L Ed 2d 343, 111 S Ct 330; *Granfinanciera, S.A. v Nordberg* (1989) 492 US 33, 106 L Ed 2d 26, 109 S Ct 2782; *In re Baker & Getty Fin. Servs., Inc.* (Rafoth v National Union Bank) (6th Cir 1992) 954 F2d 1169; *In re Kaiser Steel Corp.* (10th Cir 1990) 911 F2d 380; *In re United Missouri Bank* (8th Cir 1990) 901 F2d 1449; *In re Ben Cooper, Inc.* (2d Cir 1990) 896 F2d 1394, vacated (1991) 498 US 964, 112 L Ed

2d 408, 111 S Ct 425, reinstated (2d Cir 1991) 924 F2d 36; *In re Palomar Elec. Supply, Inc.* (SD Cal 1992) 138 BR 959; *In re Transcon Lines* (Gumport v Growth Fin. Corp.) (CD Cal 1990) 121 BR 837; *In re Interbank Mortgage Corp.* (Walsh v California Commerce Bank) (Bankr ND Cal 1991) 128 BR 269. See also *In re Lion Country Safari, Inc.* (The Splash v Irvine Co.) (Bankr CD Cal 1991) 124 BR 566 (debtor waived right to jury trial by voluntarily submitting to equitable powers of bankruptcy court when it filed its case).

Effective December 1, 1997, absent contrary congressional action, Fed R Bankr P 9015 makes certain Federal Rules of Civil Procedure regarding jury trials applicable to bankruptcy courts.

Title 28 USC §§1452(b) (remand of a removed action) and 1334(c)(2) (mandatory abstention) were amended in 1990 to clarify that the prohibition on appeals from such orders applies only to appeals to the court of appeals or Supreme Court, not to appeals from a bankruptcy court to a district court. Thus, a final order of remand or of mandatory abstention issued by a bankruptcy court is now subject to appellate review by the district court. *In re Borelli* (Dickinson v Duck) (ND Cal 1991) 132 BR 648.

In the area of appeals, the 1994 Act made two important changes. First, 28 USC §158(b) requires each circuit to establish a bankruptcy appellate panel unless the judicial council of the circuit finds there are insufficient resources in the circuit or establishment of the panel would result in undue delay or increased cost to litigants. Either party may timely object to the panel hearing the appeal, in which case the appeal will be heard by the district court. 28 USC §158(c). In addition, §158(a) has been amended to make an order extending the debtor's exclusive period under 11 USC §1121 for filing a plan of reorganization (or reducing such period) an appealable order.

[§10.5] Jurisdiction

The bankruptcy court has broad jurisdiction to determine a debtor's tax liability. 11 USC §505. However, the Ninth Circuit has held that it has no jurisdiction to determine the tax liability of a partner of the debtor. *American Principals Leasing Corp. v U.S.* (9th Cir 1990) 904 F2d 477. It has also held that a bankruptcy court is prevented by IRC §7421 (the "Anti-Injunction Act") from enjoining the IRS from collecting penalty taxes from the debtor's responsible officer. *American Bicycle Ass'n v U.S.* (9th Cir 1990) 895 F2d 1277; see also *U.S. v Hemmen* (9th Cir 1995) 51 F3d 883.

Under 28 USC §1334(b), bankruptcy courts have jurisdiction over civil proceedings "related to" a bankruptcy case. The Third Circuit has held that a proceeding is "related to a bankruptcy case if its outcome could *conceivably* affect the estate or the debtor's rights or liabilities." *Pacor,*

Inc. v Higgins (3d Cir 1984) 743 F2d 984, 994. In *In re Fietz* (9th Cir 1988) 852 F2d 455, the Ninth Circuit adopted the Third Circuit's broad interpretation of the statute. Under this test, it will be extremely difficult to argue that the bankruptcy court has no jurisdiction over a noncore proceeding. See *Kaonohi Ohana, Ltd. v Sutherland* (9th Cir 1989) 873 F2d 1302 (bankruptcy court had jurisdiction over suit between two nondebtors that might reduce one party's claim against bankruptcy estate). Recently, the Ninth Circuit held that, within the context of a debtor's attempt to enjoin an unlawful detainer action by its landlord as a violation of the automatic stay, the issue of whether the lease was the property of the estate so affected the debtor's ability to reorganize that the matter constituted a core proceeding. Virtually the entire matter arose in or under bankruptcy law. *In re Goodman* (9th Cir 1993) 991 F2d 613.

REPRESENTING INSOLVENT DEBTORS

[§10.6] Whether To File for Bankruptcy Relief; Alternatives

The cross-reference in the first paragraph of Book §10.6 should be to §9.6.

Selecting Proper Chapter; Consumer Debt

[§10.11] Straight Bankruptcy—Chapter 7

A Chapter 7 case filed by an individual may be dismissed under 11 USC §707(b), by the court on its own motion, or on a motion by the United States trustee, if the debts are primarily consumer debts and if "relief," *i.e.,* a discharge, would constitute a substantial abuse of Chapter 7. The primary factor in determining whether relief constitutes "substantial abuse" is the debtor's ability to fund a Chapter 13 plan (see Update §10.12). *Fonder v U.S.* (8th Cir 1992) 974 F2d 996; *U.S. Trustee v Harris* (8th Cir 1992) 960 F2d 74; *In re Kelly* (Zolog v Kelly) (9th Cir 1988) 841 F2d 908.

The question whether a Chapter 7 case may be dismissed when the debtor refuses to answer questions about assets or transfers based on the fifth amendment continues to come up. At least two courts have held that when a debtor's refusal to answer questions precludes the fair and effective administration of the estate, a dismissal without prejudice does not penalize the debtor for invoking the fifth amendment. See *In re Moses* (ED Mich 1992) 792 F Supp 529; *In re Fekos* (Mellon Bank v Fekos) (Bankr WD Pa 1992) 148 BR 10.

In *Dewsnup v Timm* (1992) 502 US 410, 116 L Ed 2d 903, 112 S Ct 773, the Supreme Court held that "lien stripping" is not permitted in a Chapter 7 case. The practice of "lien stripping" had been based on 11 USC §506(a) and (d). Under §506(a), an undersecured claim is split into two pieces—a secured piece limited to the value of the collateral and an unsecured piece for the balance. Section 506(d) appears to render a lien "void" to the extent that it secures a claim that "is not an allowed secured claim." Many debtors used this interpretation of the interplay between §506(a) and (d) as a basis to avoid the undersecured portion of a trust deed beneficiary's claim by obtaining a low judicially determined valuation under §506(a) and paying off the reduced amount of the claim or depriving the lienholder of any postpetition appreciation in the value of the collateral by voiding the lien.

The majority in *Dewsnup* held that using §506(d) to "lien strip" was inconsistent with pre-Code law that permitted a secured creditor's lien to pass through the case unaffected. The majority also compared the language of §506(a) to §506(d) and concluded that the term "allowed secured claim" in §506(d) has a different meaning than it does in §506(a), which focuses on the allowed amount of the claim. According to the majority, §506(d) looks to whether a claim that purports to be a secured claim is also an allowed claim. If the claim is an allowed claim, the lien is valid; if the claim is not an allowed claim, the lien is void. There was a strong dissent from Justice Scalia. *Dewsnup* has engendered much debate in the legal community and has drawn significant criticism.

A troublesome issue regarding the priority of a late-filed priority tax claim in a Chapter 7 case was recently resolved by the Ninth Circuit and the essential holding in the case was codified in the 1994 Act. In *In re Pacific Atlantic Trading Co.* (9th Cir 1994) 33 F3d 1064, the court held that late filed priority tax claims are entitled to a first priority in distribution under §726(a)(1). The 1994 Act adopts this approach. It now provides that timely and late filed priority tax claims will have the same priority if distributions to creditors have not yet started. 11 USC §726(a)(1). The 1994 Act also amends 11 USC §502(b)(9) to provide that tardiness is a ground for disallowance, subject to amended §726(a)(1) and the Federal Rules of Bankruptcy Procedure.

[§10.12] Chapter 13 Plan

The statement in Book §10.12 regarding the amount of secured and unsecured debt for an individual Chapter 13 debtor is now incorrect. The 1994 Act increased the amounts to $250,000 in unsecured debt and $750,000 in secured debt. 11 USC §109(e).

Title 11 USC §1322(c), referred to in Book §10.12, was renumbered by the 1994 Act. It is now 11 USC §1322(d).

The 1994 Act also added new 11 USC §1322(e) to overrule *Rake v Wade* (1993) 508 US 464, 124 L Ed 2d 424, 113 S Ct 2187, which held that a debtor must pay interest on interest when curing a mortgage arrearage.

A fertile ground for litigation has been whether the Chapter 13 plan has been filed in good faith. The question of good faith often arises in the context of a motion to dismiss the case because of serial filings by the debtor or a challenge to the adequacy of the proposed repayment under the plan. In *In re Eisen* (9th Cir 1994) 14 F3d 469, the court held that a petition filed in bad faith may be dismissed for cause under 11 USC §1307(c). The standard is the same as that used by courts to determine whether the plan has been proposed in good faith. Other decisions in this area include *In re Barrett* (5th Cir 1992) 964 F2d 588; *In re Love* (7th Cir 1992) 957 F2d 1350; *In re Huerta* (Bankr CD Cal 1992) 137 BR 356.

In determining good faith, the bankruptcy court must consider the totality of the circumstances. *In re Goeb* (9th Cir 1990) 675 F2d 1386. The bankruptcy court must make findings of fact to support a finding of good faith. *In re Tucker* (9th Cir 1993) 989 F2d 328. See also *In re Powers* (Bankr CD Cal 1991) 135 BR 980, holding that a creditor's failure to object to confirmation of a Chapter 13 plan did not bar a later motion to dismiss the case on the ground of bad faith at the time the petition was filed.

In *In re Beatty* (Bankr 9th Cir 1994) 162 BR 853, the Bankruptcy Appellate Panel held that the debtor may dismiss its case even after the bankruptcy court has issued an oral ruling converting the case to Chapter 7. *In re Gillead* (Bankr ED Cal 1994) 171 BR 886 held that although 11 USC §1325(b), which requires the debtor to use projected disposable income (*i.e.*, income net of living expenses) to fund payments under the plan, sets sure parameters for a determination of good faith, the statute does not specify how much or what percentage; each case must determine whether the debtor's proposed expenses are reasonable.

A so-called Chapter 20 case (a Chapter 7 followed by a Chapter 13) was approved as not violative of the Bankruptcy Code in *Johnson v Home State Bank* (1991) 501 US 78, 115 L Ed 2d 66, 111 S Ct 2150 (mortgage lien that secured obligation for which debtor's personal liability had been discharged in liquidation proceeding under Chapter 7 was claim subject to inclusion in debtor's Chapter 13 plan).

A Chapter 13 trustee may seek postconfirmation modification of the plan to increase payments. *In re Louquet* (Bankr 9th Cir 1991) 125 BR 267. The appropriate test for modification under 11 USC §1329 is discussed in *In re O'Brien* (Bankr D Ariz 1995) 181 BR 71, 78. See also *In re Powers* (Powers v Savage) (Bankr 9th Cir 1996) 202 BR 618; *In re Witkowski* (7th Cir 1994) 16 F3d 739; *In re Anderson* (9th Cir 1994) 21 F3d 355.

A Chapter 13 plan cannot include a spousal or child support debt without the claimant's consent. In *In re Pacana* (Bankr 9th Cir 1991) 125 BR 19, the Bankruptcy Appellate Panel concluded that the Bankruptcy Code excepted this type of claim from discharge and from the effect of the automatic stay. Therefore, such a claim could be enforced under state law either before or after confirmation of the Chapter 13 plan without obtaining relief from the automatic stay, even if enforcement of the claim made it impossible for the debtor to perform the plan.

Under 11 USC §1322(b)(2), a Chapter 13 debtor is prohibited from splitting an undersecured residential mortgage into a secured claim and an unsecured claim, because such bifurcation violates the language of §1322(b)(2). *Nobelman v American Sav. Bank* (1993) 508 US 324, 124 L Ed 2d 228, 113 S Ct 2106. This decision effectively eliminated "lien stripping" in Chapter 13 cases, just as *Dewsnup v Timm* (1992) 502 US 410, 116 L Ed 2d 903, 112 S Ct 773, discussed in Update §10.11, eliminated the practice in Chapter 7 cases.

In *Nobelman,* the Court focused on language in 11 USC §1322(b)(2) prohibiting modification of "the rights of holders of secured claims" if such claims are secured by the debtor's principal residence. Because one of the rights of the holder of the claim is to have the entire claim secured by the debtor's principal residence, the Court rejected the attempt to modify those rights by reducing the lien to the extent the creditor was undersecured.

The holder of a junior mortgage whose lien is valueless may, in some circumstances, have its claim modified under the Chapter 13 plan. *In re Hornes* (Bankr D Conn 1993) 160 BR 709. In *In re Geyer* (Bankr SD Cal 1996) 203 BR 726, the bankruptcy court refused to use 11 USC §1322(b)(2) to protect a creditor with a valueless lien on the debtor's residence. *In re Neverla* (Bankr WD NY 1996) 194 BR 547 reaches the opposite result.

In *In re Arvelo* (Bankr D NJ 1995) 176 BR 349, the bankruptcy court interpreted *Dewsnup*, *Nobelman*, and *Rake*, and held that interest on a mortgage arrearage may be charged only to the extent that the arrearage claim is secured as determined under §506(a). The court rejected the mortgagee's argument that its claim could be divided into its secured and unsecured components to arrive at a conclusion that the value of the property securing the claim was greater than the mortgagee's allowed secured claim, thus entitling it to pre-confirmation interest under §506(b).

The reference to Fed R Bankr P 4015 in Book §10.12 is in error. The correct reference is to Fed R Bankr P 3015.

The citation for *In re Taylor,* cited in Book §10.12, is *In re Taylor* (Bankr D Ariz 1981) 15 BR 596.

[§10.14] Dischargeable Debts

Under 11 USC §1328(a)(3), criminal fines and restitution are not dischargeable. Further, §1328(a)(2) excepts from discharge any debt for death or personal injury caused by the debtor's operation of a motor vehicle while intoxicated from using alcohol, a drug, or another substance as provided in 11 USC §523(a)(9).

In *In re Thompson* (4th Cir 1994) 16 F3d 576, the court of appeals held that costs imposed as part of a criminal conviction are not dischargeable under 11 USC §523(a)(7).

At least one court has held that *In re Petite Auberge, Inc.,* (9th Cir 1981) 650 F2d 192, cited in Book §10.14, is no longer valid. See *In re California Wholesale Elec. Co.* (Bankr CD Cal 1990) 121 BR 360. Relying on *In re Farmers Markets, Inc.* (State Bd. of Equalization v Farmers Markets, Inc.) (9th Cir 1986) 792 F2d 1400 and *U.S. v Ron Pair Enters., Inc.* (1989) 489 US 235, 103 L Ed 2d 290, 109 S Ct 1026, the court in *California Wholesale Elec.* held that the state is entitled to postpetition interest on prepetition, oversecured tax claims, but not to penalties on those claims. But see *In re Del Mission Ltd.* (Taxel v State Employment Dev. Dep't) (Bankr SD Cal 1990) 116 BR 734, which reaffirmed the validity of *Petite Auberge.*

For a case in which the court permitted an unscheduled claim to be scheduled after the bar date in order to allow the debtor to obtain a discharge of that debt, see *In re Kuhr* (Southern Pac. Land Co. v Kuhr) (Bankr ED Cal 1991) 132 BR 421.

In re Seidel (Seidel v Larson), cited in Book §10.14, has been overruled by the 1994 Act's addition of 11 USC §1322(c)(2). See *In re Miller* (Bankr SD Fla 1995) 191 BR 487; *In re Jones* (Bankr D Or 1995) 188 BR 281; *In re Chang* (Bankr ND Ill 1995) 185 BR 50.

[§10.17] Business Reorganization—Chapter 11

An individual debtor is eligible to reorganize under Chapter 11 even though the debtor is not engaged in business. *Toibb v Radloff* (1991) 501 US 157, 115 L Ed 2d 145, 111 S Ct 2197. The Court relied principally on the plain language of 11 USC §109 to support its decision.

The 1994 Act added a new definition of "small business." 11 USC §101(51C). A small business includes a person engaged in commercial or business activities, except primarily owning or operating real property, whose secured and unsecured debts do not exceed $2 million. Changes to Chapter 11 to accommodate debtors electing treatment as a small business include discretionary elimination of the creditors' committee (§1102(a)(3)) and shorter time periods for filing plans for both the debtor (100 days) and others (160 days) (§1122(e)).

The 1994 Act added 11 USC §1122(b)(5), restricting an individual debtor's ability to modify the rights of a creditor whose claim is secured only by the debtor's principal residence. This conforms Chapter 11 to Chapter 13. See 11 USC §1322(b)(2).

In 1993, the Ninth Circuit became the first circuit-level court to hold that the "new value" exception to the absolute priority rule survived the enactment of the Bankruptcy Code in 1978. *In re Bonner Mall Partnership* (Bonner Mall Partnership v U.S. Bancorp Mortgage Co.) (9th Cir 1993)

2 F3d 899. In a "cramdown," a plan of reorganization can be confirmed over the no vote of an impaired class as long as dissenting impaired classes receive "fair and equitable" treatment under the plan. What is "fair and equitable" is determined by 11 USC §§1129(b)(2)(A), (B), and (C). Regarding a dissenting class of unsecured creditors, 11 USC §1129(b)(2)(B) provides that unless each holder of a claim is paid in full, junior claims or interests (which usually means existing equity interests, *i.e.,* the owners) cannot receive or retain any property under the plan "on account" of such junior claims or interests.

The new value exception allows the shareholders of a corporation in bankruptcy to obtain an interest in the reorganized debtor in exchange for new capital contributions over the objections of a class of creditors that has not received full payment on its claims. In *Bonner Mall,* the Ninth Circuit concluded that the exception was not overruled by Congress when it passed 11 USC §1129(b). The Ninth Circuit held that if the equity holders contribute cash or cash equivalents to the reorganized debtor under the plan in exchange for a continued ownership interest in the debtor, the value given to the contributors is not given "on account" of the old junior claim or interest, but instead is given "on account" of the new equity contribution.

What constitutes new value is still an open question. Generally, there are five recognized elements: the value given by existing equity holders must be (1) new, (2) substantial, (3) money or money's worth, (4) necessary for a successful reorganization, and (5) reasonably equivalent to the value or interest received. *Case v Los Angeles Lumber* (1939) 308 US 106, 84 L Ed 110, 60 S Ct 1. For a recent case that exemplifies the hostility of some courts to single asset real estate debtors trying to keep the secured creditor captive to an undercollateralized loan through a combination of claim classification and insufficient new value, see *In re Dollar Assocs.* (Bankr ND Cal 1994) 172 BR 945. For discussion of relief from automatic stay in cases involving "single asset real estate," see Update §10.27.

Another battleground in the cramdown area has been the classification and treatment of claims in order to obtain the accepting impaired class of claims required for confirmation under 11 USC §1129(a)(10). Impairment is defined in 11 USC §1124. In general, a claim is impaired if the plan changes the legal, equitable or contractual rights of the holder of the claim. This dispute usually arises in the single asset real estate case in which the major secured creditor is undersecured. Under 11 USC §506(a), the creditor's claim is bifurcated into a secured piece and an unsecured piece. If the unsecured piece of the claim is large enough, a no vote by the creditor on that portion of its claim will dominate the unsecured creditor class and deprive the debtor of an accepting impaired class and the debtor will be unable to meet the confirmation requirement of 11 USC §1129(a)(10). Given the nature of most single asset real estate cases, the creditor ordinarily votes no on the treatment of the secured portion of its claim as well.

To avoid this dilemma, the debtor might try to place the unsecured portion of the creditor's claim in a different class from other unsecured creditors. Although similar claims may be placed in different classes, the classification must be for a legitimate purpose. *In re Barakat* (Barakat v Life Ins. Co.) (9th Cir 1996) 99 F3d 1520; *In re Tucson Self-Storage, Inc.* (Bankr 9th Cir 1994) 166 BR 892; *In re Johnston* (Steelcase, Inc. v Johnston) (Bankr 9th Cir 1992) 140 BR 526, aff'd (9th Cir 1994) 21 F3d 323.

Most courts hold that isolating the deficiency claim from other general unsecured claims in order to obtain an affirmative vote for the plan is impermissible gerrymandering. See *In re Boston Post Rd. Ltd. Partnership* (2d Cir 1994) 21 F3d 477; *John Hancock Mut. Life Ins. Co. v Route 37 Business Park Assoc.* (3d Cir 1993) 987 F2d 154; *In re Bryson Prop., XVIII* (Travelers Ins. Co. v Bryson Prop., XVIII) (4th Cir 1992) 961 F2d 496; *In re Greystone III Joint Venture* (Phoenix Mut. Life Ins. Co. v Greystone III Joint Venture) (5th Cir 1991) 948 F2d 134, as amended following reh'g 995 F2d 1274.

One recent case rejecting the propriety of separate classification of the unsecured deficiency claim is *In re Moorpark Adventure* (Bankr ED Cal 1993) 161 BR 254. See also *In re D & W Realty Corp.* (SD NY 1994) 165 BR 127; but see *In re Woodbrook Assocs.* (7th Cir 1994) 19 F3d 312; *In re Baldwin Towne Ctr., Ltd.* (Bankr CD Cal 1994) 171 BR 374.

The second context in which the classification and treatment of claims becomes a focal point for dispute is when a class of claims is "artificially" impaired in order to obtain an accepting impaired class under 11 USC §1129(a)(10). As in the gerrymandering cases, the dispute normally arises in the single asset real estate case, in which either the secured creditor is fully secured or elects to be treated as fully secured under 11 USC §1111(b)(2), or the deficiency claim of the undersecured creditor has been classified separately from other unsecured claims. In order to have the required accepting impaired class, the debtor might impair the general unsecured creditor class by delaying payment to that class until 60 days after confirmation of the plan. At least one circuit court has held that "artificial impairment" is improper when the class is impaired at the discretion of a debtor who clearly has the ability to treat the class otherwise. See *In re Windsor on the River Assocs., Ltd.* (8th Cir 1993) 7 F3d 127. See also *In re Investors Florida Aggressive Growth Fund, Ltd.* (Bankr ND Fla 1994) 168 BR 760; *In re Kellogg Square Partnership* (Bankr D Minn 1993) 160 BR 343; *In re Landing Assocs., Ltd.* (Bankr WD Tex 1993) 157 BR 791.

A third recent battleground in the cramdown wars is the appropriate interest rate to be used in nonconsensual plans. In this regard, the "fair and equitable" requirement of 11 USC §1129(b)(2)(A)(i)(II) requires a dissenting secured creditor to retain its lien on its collateral and receive deferred cash payments having a present value equal to the value of the secured creditor's interest in its collateral. When the creditor is undersecured and its claim has been bifurcated into a secured piece and an unsecured piece, the amount of the secured claim will be equal to the value of the collateral.

The interest rate is important to both the debtor and the creditor. The creditor will want as high a rate as possible. The debtor will want the lowest rate possible. Generally, two tests have been developed for determining the appropriate rate: the market rate approach and the risk-adjusted approach. The market rate approach requires the proponent to present evidence regarding the interest rate available in the market to a borrower with the debtor's characteristics, taking into account such factors as the condition of the security and the proposed length of the loan. One acknowledged problem with the market rate approach is that when the creditor is undersecured and its claim is bifurcated into secured and unsecured pieces, the secured piece is equal to the value of the collateral. This means that the equivalent loan in the market would have a 100-percent loan-to-value ratio, a loan that no lender would ever voluntarily make. When applying the risk-adjusted approach, the proponent starts with a "risk-less" or "risk-free" rate and adds or subtracts basis points. The risk-free rate is ordinarily the rate of interest paid on obligations of the United States Treasury for investments of duration comparable to the term of the debt under the plan.

Some courts use a hybrid of the above two approaches by building a risk-adjusted rate and testing it against the market. Still other courts use a split loan approach by taking the first 70 percent of the debt and calculating an interest rate for a 70-percent loan-to-value loan and then taking the remaining debt and calculating a rate of interest for a 100-percent loan-to-value loan and blending the two rates to reach a single rate. Other courts view the last tier of the debt as "equity" and calculate the equivalent of a desired return for an investor.

In the Ninth Circuit, the risk-adjusted approach has been followed. *In re Fowler* (Farm Credit Bank v Fowler) (9th Cir 1990) 903 F2d 694. See also *In re Boulders on the River, Inc.* (Pacific First Bank v Boulders on the River, Inc.) (Bankr 9th Cir 1994) 164 BR 99; *In re Villa Diablo Assocs.* (Bankr ND Cal 1993) 156 BR 650. Determination of the appropriate interest rate is done on a case-by-case basis. *In re Camino Real Landscape Maintenance Contractors, Inc.* (U.S. v Camino Real Landscape Maintenance Contractors, Inc.) (9th Cir 1987) 818 F2d 1503.

[§10.18] What To File To Start a Bankruptcy Case

Except in a Chapter 9 municipality case, the debtor, unless the court orders otherwise, must file schedules of assets and liabilities, a schedule of current income and expenses, a schedule of executory contracts and unexpired leases, and a statement of financial affairs. Fed R Bankr P 1007(b)(1).

An individual debtor in a Chapter 7 case with secured consumer debts must also file a statement indicating whether the debtor intends (1) to "redeem" encumbered property (by paying the debt to the extent of the value of the property), (2) to claim the property as exempt and "avoid" the lien, or (3) to abandon the property to the secured creditor. This intention must be performed within 45 days. 11 USC §§521(2), 722; Fed R Bankr P 1007(b)(2).

The filing fees for Chapters 7, 11, and 13 were increased in 1993. See 28 USC §1930(a). The fee for Chapter 7 and 13 cases is now $130. The fee for Chapter 11 cases is now $800. In addition, quarterly maintenance fees must be paid to the Office of the United States Trustee. The amount of the fees is based on the total disbursements made during the quarter. There is a minimum fee of $250 per quarter, escalating to $10,000 depending on the total disbursements for the quarter. These fees are used to fund the United States trustee program. See Update §10.2.

[§10.19] Payment of Attorneys' Fees

The employment of professionals, including attorneys, in bankruptcy cases is governed by 11 USC §327. Title 11 USC §§328–330 deal with compensation of professionals. Generally, an attorney for a debtor or trustee must be appointed by the court (11 USC §327) and will be paid only after approval by the court pursuant to the standards in 11 USC §330.

An application from a debtor, trustee, or creditors' committee to employ an attorney must disclose any proposed arrangement for compensation. The application must be accompanied by a verified statement of the attorney's connections with the debtor, creditors, other parties in interest, their respective attorneys and accountants, the United States trustee, or any person employed in the office of the United States trustee. Fed R Bankr P 2014(a).

Counsel for the debtor may not hold an interest adverse to the estate and must be a "disinterested person." 11 USC §327(a). Title 11 USC §101(14) defines "disinterested person." An attorney who is a creditor of the debtor is not disinterested and is prohibited from representing the debtor. See, *e.g., In re Siliconix, Inc.* (ND Cal 1991) 135 BR 378 (employment of accountant rejected because of existence of prepetition claim for fees). See also *U.S. Trustee v Price Waterhouse* (3d Cir 1994) 19 F3d 138 (disinterestedness is an absolute requirement for professionals, without exception).

Failure to be completely candid, even through ignorance, may result in complete disallowance of fees. See *In re American Thrift & Loan Ass'n* (Bankr SD Cal 1992) 137 BR 381. See also *In re Envirodyne Indus., Inc.* (Bankr ND Ill 1993) 150 BR 1008, in which the order approving counsel's employment was vacated because counsel failed to disclose obvious conflicts to the court.

In *In re Weibel, Inc.* (McCutchen, Doyle, Brown & Enersen v Official Comm. of Unsecured Creditors) (Bankr 9th Cir 1994) 176 BR 209, the bankruptcy appellate panel upheld the refusal of the bankruptcy court to employ counsel on the ground that one of the law firm's partners had been a director of the debtor and was thus not disinterested. The firm also was denied any compensation on the basis of quantum meruit because the court found that the Bankruptcy Code "does not provide for fee awards based on state law theories such as *quantum meruit.*" 176 BR at 212. For a case distinguishing *Weibel*, see *In re CIC Inv. Corp.* (First Interstate Bank of Nevada v CIC Inv. Corp.) (Bankr 9th Cir 1996) 192 BR 549.

Failure to promptly seek court approval of employment can result in denial of fees incurred before entry of an order. There is a strong reluctance by courts to approve retroactive or *nunc pro tunc* employment applications. See *In re THC Fin. Corp.* (9th Cir 1988) 837 F2d 389; *In re Shirley* (Bankr 9th Cir 1992) 134 BR 940; *In re Downtown Inv. Club* (Bankr 9th Cir 1988) 89 BR 59. But see *In re Atkins* (Atkins v Wain, Samuel & Co.) (9th Cir 1995) 69 F3d 970, in which exceptional circumstances justified a *nunc pro tunc* order authorizing employment of accountants and awarding fees.

Title 11 USC §330(a)(5) contains a disgorgement provision if any interim fees paid to a professional are later disallowed when final application is made. See *In re Occidental Fin. Group, Inc.* (9th Cir 1994) 40 F3d 1059; *In re CF Holding Corp.* (Bankr D Conn 1994) 164 BR 799.

In Chapter 12 and 13 cases, §330(a)(4)(B) provides that a debtor's counsel may be compensated from the estate for representing the interests of the debtor based on a consideration of the benefit and necessity of such services and the other factors set forth in §330. The failure to list a Chapter 7 debtor's counsel in this subsection and the deletion of some of the language in the prior version of §330(a) raises the question whether anything done by debtor's counsel in a Chapter 7 case will be compensable.

Every attorney for a debtor, regardless of whether the attorney applies for compensation, must file a statement of compensation that has been paid or promised within one year of the filing of the bankruptcy case. The statement must be filed within 15 days after the case begins. Supplemental statements must be filed within 15 days if any new payments are made or promised. Fed R Bankr P 2016(b).

An application for payment must describe with specificity what work was performed by the attorney. The standard of 11 USC §330(a)(1) is "reasonable compensation for actual, necessary services rendered." Wasteful or unnecessary services are not compensable. See *In re Xebec* (Bankr 9th Cir 1992) 147 BR 518; *In re Kitchen Factors, Inc.* (Bankr 9th Cir 1992) 143 BR 560. Section 330(a)(2) lists a set of factors for the court to consider in determining the appropriate amount of compensation. These factors include the time spent on the services; the rates charged; whether the services were necessary to the administration of, or beneficial at the time at which the service was rendered toward the completion of the case; whether the services were performed within a reasonable amount of time commensurate with the complexity, importance, and nature of the problem; and whether the compensation is reasonable based on the customary compensation charged by comparably skilled practitioners in nonbankruptcy cases. The section provides that compensation should not be allowed for unnecessary duplication of services or services not reasonably likely to benefit the debtor's estate or not necessary to the administration of the estate.

The ordinary, but not necessarily exclusive, means of calculating a reasonable fee is the "lodestar" method, *i.e.,* a reasonable hourly rate multiplied by a reasonable number of hours. See *Unsecured Creditors Comm. v Puget Sound Plywood, Inc.* (9th Cir 1991) 924 F2d 955; *In re Manoa Fin. Co.* (9th Cir 1988) 853 F2d 687.

The lodestar approach, however, is not the exclusive method for determining compensation. Contingent fee arrangements are permitted. *In re Reimers* (9th Cir 1992) 972 F2d 1127. In some cases, a contingent fee award more accurately reflects the benefit provided by counsel to the estate. See *Unsecured Creditors Comm. v Puget Sound Plywood, Inc., supra*; *In re Kitchen Factors, Inc., supra.*

Counsel must also consult the local fee guidelines promulgated by the United States trustee and/or adopted by the judges of the bankruptcy court for the proper formatting of the fee application. Project billing is required by some guidelines, and clumping of time is sometimes considered objectionable. Overhead items such as word processing are normally not reimbursed. Photocopy and telecopy charges are generally reimbursed at actual cost. See generally *In re Pothoven* (Bankr SD Iowa 1988) 84 BR 579 (disallowance of overhead expenses).

It has been well established in the Ninth Circuit that compensation is allowed for the time spent in preparation of the fee application. *In re NuCorp Energy, Inc.* (9th Cir 1985) 764 F2d 655. The 1994 Act added §330(a)(6), expressly authorizing reasonable compensation for the preparation of a fee application. Most jurisdictions, including most bankruptcy courts in California, require specificity in fee applications and might disapprove a portion of the fees requested if the application is too vague. *In re Whet, Inc.* (Bankr D Mass 1986) 61 BR 709.

In *In re Riverside-Linden Inv. Co.* (Boldt v Crake) (9th Cir 1991) 925 F2d 320, 324, the court held that interest accrues on attorney fees only from the date the court awards them. This is another reason why attorneys representing debtors, trustees, and creditors' committees might wish to apply for approval of their fees promptly after the service is performed, even though funds are not currently available to pay them.

As long as a secured creditor has an attorney fees clause in its loan documents, the creditor is entitled to a reasonable fee from its collateral (assuming the creditor is oversecured), regardless of whether it was the "prevailing party." *In re McGaw Prop. Mgmt., Inc.* (Bankr CD Cal 1991) 133 BR 227, citing *In re 268, Ltd.* (9th Cir 1986) 789 F2d 674 and *In re Dalessio* (Bankr 9th Cir 1987) 74 BR 721.

The discussion in Book §10.19 regarding the payment and treatment of retainers may no longer be valid. Several bankruptcy courts have held that retainers (other than flat fee retainers) are property of the estate and must be held in a client trust account until a fee application has been filed and approved. See *In re Hathaway Ranch Partnership* (Bankr CD Cal 1990) 116 BR 208, 218; *In re McDonald Bros. Constr., Inc.* (Bankr ND Ill 1990) 114 BR 989, 993 n1; *In re C & P Auto Transport, Inc.* (Bankr ED Cal 1988) 94 BR 682.

[§10.20] Debtor's Exemption Rights

The 1994 Act doubled the federal exemptions contained in 11 USC §522(d). California has opted out of the federal exemptions (see CCP §703.130), and has its own set of exemptions applicable in bankruptcy cases in lieu of the otherwise applicable state exemptions (see CCP §703.140). These alternative exemptions now lag behind the §522(d) exemptions.

Code of Civil Procedure §703.140 has been amended to provide that all the exemptions under CCP §§703.010–704.995, *including the homestead exemption,* are available to the debtor, regardless of whether there is a money judgment against the debtor or the judgment is being enforced by execution sale or other procedure. See *In re Pladson* (Kendall v Pladson) (9th Cir 1994) 35 F3d 462.

For discussion of liens that impair exemptions, see §10.55.

A trustee's failure to object to a debtor's claim of a homestead exemption does not bind the trustee to the debtor's valuation of the real property. The trustee is entitled to sell the real property claimed as exempt and realize any value in the property over the amount of the homestead exemption even if this surplus reflects postpetition appreciation. See *In re Hyman* (Hyman v Plotkin) (9th Cir 1992) 967 F2d 1316. See also *In re Canino* (Canino v Bleau) (Bankr 9th Cir 1995) 185 BR 584.

A trustee can sell a homestead owned by a debtor and a nondebtor spouse as their separate property under 11 USC §363(h). The estate is entitled to any surplus from the debtor's share of the sale proceeds over the amount of the debtor's homestead exemption. *In re Reed* (9th Cir 1991) 940 F2d 1317. By contrast, under state law, a creditor with a judgment against only one spouse might be unable to obtain an execution sale of the same homestead. State law permits an execution sale of a homestead only if the sale price is sufficient to pay all liens against the property and the debtor's homestead exemption. CCP §704.800. However, under CCP §704.820, only the judgment debtor's share of the property can be sold. Nevertheless, the sale price must exceed the debtor's homestead exemption and the full amount of the liens against the property. *Schoenfeld v Norberg* (1970) 11 CA3d 755, 90 CR 47.

If a debtor claims an exemption without legal basis and no timely objection is made, the debtor can keep the exemption. *Taylor v Freeland & Kronz* (1992) 503 US 638, 118 L Ed 2d 280, 112 S Ct 1644. The Court observed there are sanctions for fraud and concealment that will curtail debtor abuse and afford relief when necessary. See also *In re Green* (11th Cir 1994) 31 F3d 1098, where the trustee failed to challenge the debtor's "one dollar" valuation of a personal injury claim that later paid $15,000. The bankruptcy court refused to exempt the $15,000, but the district court reversed and the court of appeals affirmed. The entire recovery was exempt. The burden was on the trustee to file a timely objection to the exemption. But see *In re Morgan* (Bankr 9th Cir 1993) 149 BR 147, discussed in Update §10.55.

In *In re Glass* (Bankr 9th Cir 1995) 60 F3d 565, the Ninth Circuit Court of Appeals held that the debtor could not claim an exemption in property voluntarily reconveyed to him by his son following the trustee's informal questioning of the prepetition transfer of the property of the father/debtor to the son for no consideration. Under 11 USC §522(g), the debtor's ability to exempt recovered property is limited. No formal action to recover the property by the trustee is required to trigger §522(g).

For a discussion of the treatment of ERISA and similar plans in bankruptcy, see Update §9.27A.

[§10.21] Converting Nonexempt Property to Exempt

The Ninth Circuit limited the debtor's ability to convert the equity in his home into an exempt annuity purchased with the proceeds of a home equity loan by limiting the exemption to the amount reasonably necessary to support the debtor. *In re Moffat* (9th Cir 1992) 959 F2d 740. The debtor in *Moffat* tried to claim the entire annuity as exempt as an unmatured life insurance policy, but the court ruled the policy was matured and therefore limited the exemption under CCP §704.100(c). But see *In re Hill* (Bankr ND Fla 1994) 163 BR 598, where the debtor successfully shielded $650,000 by purchasing a homestead in Florida shortly after entry of $15 million judgment against him. There was no evidence of specific intent to defraud creditors.

[§10.22] Election of Federal or State Exemptions

The California exemption scheme for debtors in bankruptcy cases (CCP §§703.110–703.140) has been upheld as constitutional. This exemption scheme was also held to require joint debtors, *i.e.,* husband and wife, to share a set of exemptions, rather than each claiming the full exemption amount permitted an individual debtor. *Baldwin v Marshack* (Bankr 9th Cir 1987) 70 BR 612. The court rejected arguments that the statute was void for vagueness and that it denied equal protection of the law by arbitrarily discriminating against married couples.

The amount of the exemptions allowed under 11 USC §522 does not affect the amount allowed under state law. *In re Taylor* (9th Cir 1988) 861 F2d 550 (ruling on debtor's exemptions under Montana law).

On the availability of the homestead exemption in bankruptcy, see Update §10.20.

[§10.24] Reaffirmation

The 1994 Act has added conditions to obtaining a valid reaffirmation agreement under 11 USC §524(c)–(d). The reaffirmation agreement must now contain a clear and conspicuous statement advising the debtor that the agreement is not required. 11 USC §524(c)(2)(B). The declaration of the debtor's attorney must now include a statement that the debtor has been fully advised of the legal effect and consequences of the agreement and any default under it. 11 USC §524(c)(3)(C). If the debt is a consumer debt not secured by real property and the debtor is not represented by counsel during the course of negotiating a reaffirmation agreement, the court must hold a hearing at which it will make the determination required by 11 USC §524(c)(6) (no undue hardship, best interest of the debtor). 11 USC §524(d).

[§10.26] Married Debtors

For an extensive treatment of family law issues in bankruptcy cases, see Sommer, McGarity & King, Collier Family Law and the Bankruptcy Code (1991).

Relief Available to Debtors

[§10.27] Automatic Stay

The 1994 Act made several changes to the automatic stay. First, 11 USC §362(b)(3) permits a secured creditor to take steps under state law, such as filing a continuation statement with the office of the secretary of state, to maintain the perfection of its interest without violating the stay.

Second, 11 USC §362(b)(9) is expanded to permit a taxing authority to determine a tax liability, conduct a tax audit, demand tax returns, assess a tax, or issue a notice and demand for payment without violating the stay.

Third, 11 USC §362(b)(18) now enables local governments to create or perfect statutory property tax liens for taxes that accrue after the petition date without violating the stay. This last change overrules *In re Glasply Marine Indus. Inc.* (9th Cir 1992) 971 F2d 391.

Fourth, newly added 11 USC §362(d)(3) allows the lifting of the stay in a case involving "single asset real estate" unless, within 90 days of the petition date, the debtor files a plan that has a "reasonable possibility" of being confirmed within a reasonable time, or has commenced making monthly payments to secured creditors in an amount equal to interest at a current fair market rate on the value of the creditor's interest in the property. The 90-day time period may be extended for cause. "Single asset real estate" is defined in 11 USC §101(51B).

Fifth, 11 USC §362(e) has been amended to provide that the final hearing on a motion to lift the automatic stay must be concluded within 30 days of the conclusion of the preliminary hearing, unless the parties consent to an extension or the court determines that an extension for a specific time period is required by compelling circumstances. Prior law required the final hearing to begin within 30 days of the conclusion of the preliminary hearing, but did not fix a time for the conclusion of the final hearing.

Cancellation of a contract with the debtor without first obtaining relief from the automatic stay may subject the creditor to monetary damages. See *In re Computer Communications, Inc.* (Computer Communications, Inc. v Codex Corp.) (9th Cir 1987) 824 F2d 725. Acts taken in violation of the automatic stay of 11 USC §362(a) are void, not voidable. *In re Schwartz* (9th Cir 1992) 954 F2d 569.

The automatic stay bars the filing of a legal action against the debtor on a prepetition debt even if the action is filed in bankruptcy court. *In re Penney* (Bankr ND Cal 1987) 76 BR 160. But see *In re North Coast Village, Ltd.* (Bankr 9th Cir 1992) 135 BR 641, which holds that the automatic stay does not prevent the commencement of an adversary proceeding against the debtor in the "home" bankruptcy court. The bankruptcy court can regulate the conduct of the action in order to protect the debtor.

[§10.28] Protection of Secured Creditor During Stay

The rule established by the Ninth Circuit in *In re American Mariner Indus., Inc.* (Crocker Nat'l Bank v American Mariner Indus., Inc.) (9th Cir 1984) 734 F2d 426, cited in Book §10.28, granting interest payments to undersecured creditors in exchange for keeping the automatic stay in effect, was reversed by the United States Supreme Court in *United Sav. Ass'n v Timbers of Inwood Forest Assocs., Ltd.* (1988) 484 US 365, 98 L Ed 2d 740, 108 S Ct 626. The Court reasoned that *American Mariner*'s requirement of compensation was inconsistent with 11 USC §§362(d), 506(a)–(b), and 552. Most bankruptcy courts in the Ninth Circuit are interpreting *Timbers* to mean that relief, *i.e.,* cash payments to compensate the creditor for the delay in enforcing its rights and the effects of the case on its collateral, or the lifting of the automatic stay, will be granted only if the value of the collateral is decreasing, the amount of the senior liens is increasing, or there is no prospect of the debtor's rehabilitation within a reasonable time.

Section 362(d)(3), added by the 1994 Act, seems to be a partial codification of *Timbers*, especially the requirement that there be a reasonable likelihood that there will be a successful reorganization in a reasonable period of time. However, the market interest payment requirement of 11 USC §362(d)(3)(B) looks suspiciously like the return of *American Mariner.*

Until recently, when a mortgagor of rent generating real property filed a bankruptcy petition, the status of the mortgagee's security interest in assigned rents was unclear unless a receiver had been appointed before the filing of the petition. Some courts held that the mortgagee had no interest in the rents. *In re Multi-Group III Ltd.* (Bankr D Ariz 1989) 99 BR 5. Others permitted a mortgagee to perfect its security interest postpetition by giving notice under 11 USC §546(b). *In re American Continental Corp.* (Bankr D Ariz 1989) 105 BR 564.

The 1994 Act amended 11 USC §546(b) to permit certain postpetition actions by secured creditors to maintain or accomplish perfection of their security interests. It now provides, in general, that if state law requires seizure or commencement of an action to perfect an interest, and the property has not been seized or the action commenced prepetition, perfection may be accomplished by giving notice to the debtor.

Amendments to 11 USC §363(a) in the 1994 Act have resolved the controversy over whether hotel room revenues are "rents" covered by the lender's deed of trust and assignment of rents or whether they are accounts receivable not so covered. Fees, charges, and accounts for the use or occupancy of rooms in hotels, motels, or other lodging properties are now "cash collateral" under 11 USC §363(a). Amended 11 USC §522(b)(2) makes clear that the lender's prepetition security interest will extend to postpetition hotel revenues. (The Ninth Circuit had decided this issue in favor of treating room revenues as rents and not after-acquired accounts receivable in *In re Days California Riverside Partnership* (9th Cir 1994) 27 F3d 374.)

There is an ongoing debate in cases involving income-producing real property over whether use of the rents to maintain the property constitutes adequate protection of the creditor's interest so that excess rents may be used by the debtor over the creditor's objection, and whether the accumulating rents constitute a separate fund of collateral that is entitled to adequate protection in addition to the creditor's interest in the underlying real property. Compare *In re River Oaks Ltd. Partnership* (ED Mich 1994) 166 BR 94 and *In re May* (Bankr SD Ga 1994) 169 BR 462 with *In re Mullen* (Bankr D Mass 1994) 172 BR 473.

[§10.30] Damages for Violation of Stay

Only an individual, as opposed to a corporation, may obtain damages for a willful violation of the automatic stay under 11 USC §362(h). *In re Goodman* (9th Cir 1993) 991 F2d 613. The court in *Goodman,* however, made it clear that the bankruptcy court could still assess damages as a civil contempt against the person or entity that violates the automatic stay. This ruling is consistent with Second Circuit decisions in *In re Chateaugay Corp.* (Maritime Asbestosis Legal Clinic v LTV Steel) (2d Cir 1990) 920 F2d 183 and *Fidelity Mortgage Invs. v Camelia Bldrs., Inc.* (2d Cir 1976) 550 F2d 47.

In *In re Pace* (Havelock v Taxel) (9th Cir 1995) 56 F3d 1170, the court considered whether a bankruptcy trustee who functions as the representative of the estate under 11 USC §323(a) is an individual for purposes of 11 USC §362(h). The court held that because the trustee was an individual, the trustee was entitled to damages under §362(h).

[§10.31] Effect of Discharge on Collection Judgments

When a debtor fails to list a known creditor in his or her schedules, a judgment obtained by the creditor during the case is unaffected by the automatic stay and is enforceable after the debtor receives his or her discharge. *Tarakjian v Krone* (1987) 196 CA3d 1243, 242 CR 435. The debt may be discharged, however, if the creditor had actual, timely notice of the bankruptcy case. See Update §10.36.

The 1994 Act made some technical changes to reaffirmation agreements under 11 USC §524(c) regarding disclosures to the reaffirming debtor. The 1994 Act also contains a trust fund mechanism in new §524(g) for enjoining postdischarge claims in asbestos cases.

A discharge in bankruptcy voids a judgment lien only to the extent of the debtor's personal liability. A discharge does not affect a judgment to the extent it supports a lien perfected before bankruptcy, unless the debtor has obtained an order in the bankruptcy proceeding avoiding the lien. *Songer v Cooney* (1989) 214 CA3d 387, 264 CR 1.

Despite 11 USC §524(a), an action can be filed postdischarge against a debtor to collect on an insurance policy, but not to enforce a judgment against the debtor. *In re Beeny* (Bankr 9th Cir 1992) 142 BR 360, 362; *Green v Welsh* (2d Cir 1992) 956 F2d 30, 32. But see *In re Lundberg*

(Bankr ED Okla 1993) 152 BR 316, which held that when the debtor obtained its discharge, the debt was discharged. Thus, the insurer whose liability was based on the debtor's liability was no longer liable. The court declined to apply 11 USC §524(e) to preserve the creditor's claim against the insurance company, holding that §524(e) applies only to codebtors and guarantors charged with primary liability for a debt.

In *In re Siragusa* (9th Cir 1994) 27 F3d 406, the Ninth Circuit held that postdischarge modification of alimony payments to remedy the discharge of the debtor's obligations to his ex-spouse under a prepetition property settlement did not violate the 11 USC §524(a) injunction. The amount of alimony is a state law issue and modification based upon the loss of the property settlement would be appropriate.

[§10.32] Nondischargeable Debts

The 1994 Act added some new nondischargeable debts. Title 11 USC §523(a)(14) makes debts that are incurred to pay taxes nondischargeable. Section 523(a)(15) makes nondischargeable some debts arising out of a divorce decree or separation agreement besides those that are for alimony, maintenance, or support which are nondischargeable under 11 USC §523(a)(5). These obligations are nondischargeable when the debtor has the ability to pay them and the detriment to the nondebtor spouse from the nonpayment outweighs the benefit to the debtor of discharging such debts. The debt will be *dischargeable* if paying the debt would reduce the debtor's income below that necessary for the support of the debtor and his or her dependents. According to the legislative history, §523(a)(15) is designed to address situations where divorcing spouses have agreed to make payments of marital debts as part of the marital settlement, such that one spouse agrees to pay a specific debt and hold the other spouse harmless in exchange for a reduction in alimony payments or the divorcing spouses have agreed to lower alimony payments based on a larger property settlement. Section 523(a)(15) must be raised by adversary complaint within the time required under the Federal Rules of Bankruptcy Procedure. See *In re Adams* (Beasley v Adams) (ND Ill 1996) 200 BR 630; *In re Gamble* (Gamble v Gamble) (Bankr ND Tex 1996) 196 BR 54.

Section 523(a)(16) makes postpetition condominium or cooperative apartment association dues nondischargeable so long as and for the period that the debtor actually occupied the dwelling unit or the debtor rented the unit to a tenant and received rent from the tenant. Section 523(a)(16) makes clear that prepetition dues are dischargeable. Section 523(a)(2)(C) has also been amended to extend from 40 to 60 days the presumption that debts for "luxury goods or services" incurred before bankruptcy are nondischargeable.

A claim that a debt in a Chapter 7 case is nondischargeable under 11 USC §523(a)(2)(A) (debts incurred through fraud or false pretenses) need only be proved by a preponderance of the evidence. *Grogan v Garner* (1991) 498 US 279, 112 L Ed 2d 755, 111 S Ct 654. *Grogan* is applied retroactively to proceedings pending when *Grogan* was decided. *Melton v Moore* (9th Cir 1992) 964 F2d 880. Before *Grogan,* some courts, including some in the Ninth Circuit, had required proof by clear and convincing evidence. See, *e.g., In re Dougherty* (Citibank South Dakota v Dougherty) (Bankr 9th Cir 1988) 84 BR 653.

Because a state court fraud judgment, based on a preponderance of the evidence, will now collaterally estop relitigation of the issue in bankruptcy court, it will be easier to obtain a judgment of nondischargeability based on a state court judgment of fraud. In light of the Supreme Court's rationale in *Grogan,* it is likely that the same standard will now be required for nondischargeability actions brought under 11 USC §§523(a)(2), (a)(4), and (a)(6) and for objections to discharge brought under 11 USC §727(a). See *In re Serafini* (10th Cir 1991) 938 F2d 1156.

As to the collateral estoppel effect to be given to a state court *default* judgment for fraud in a subsequent nondischargeability action under §523(a)(2)(A), see *In re Nourbakhsh* (Gayden v Nourbakhsh) (Bankr 9th Cir 1994) 162 BR 841, aff'd (9th Cir 1995) 67 F3d 798. In *Nourbakhsh,* the Ninth Circuit held that a default judgment (entered in Florida) could be domesticated in California and given collateral estoppel effect in the nondischargeability action.

A creditor seeking a determination of nondischargeability against a married debtor whose spouse is not also a debtor need not join the nondebtor spouse in the action. The issue of whether the claim is a community claim entitled to be enforced against community property can be raised in state court when the creditor attempts to execute its nondischargeable judgment. *In re Maready* (Case v Maready) (Bankr 9th Cir 1991) 122 BR 378.

Because taxes assessed more than 240 days before a bankruptcy petition is filed are dischargeable (see 11 USC §§507(a)(7)(A) and 523(a)(1)), determining the precise date of assessment is critical when counseling a potential debtor with tax debt. A state income tax is *assessed* when the assessment becomes final, not when the Notice of Additional Tax or Deficiency is issued. *In re King* (Franchise Tax Bd. v King) (Bankr 9th Cir 1991) 122 BR 383.

A debt that is not scheduled is not discharged under 11 USC §523(a)(3)(A) unless the creditor obtained actual knowledge of the bankruptcy case in time to file a proof of claim, regardless of whether any assets were distributed to creditors. *In re Bosse* (Bankr CD Cal 1991) 122 BR 410. The court in *Bosse* followed *In re Laczko* (Bankr 9th Cir 1984) 37 BR 676, aff'd (9th Cir 1985) 772 F2d 912 (unpublished opinion). But see *In re Beezly* (9th Cir 1993) 994 F2d 1433, which held that reopening a no-asset Chapter 7 case to list an unscheduled claim in order to discharge it is a futile act, because in a no-asset case, absent knowledge of the case by the creditor, the discharge is not affected by listing the claim. Instead, the question of whether the debt is discharged is determined by the nature of the claim and whether it falls under 11 USC §523(a)(3)(A) or (B). This complex and well reasoned holding is fully explained in Justice O'Scannlain's concurring opinion. For further discussion of the rights of unscheduled creditors with notice of the debtor's bankruptcy, see Update §10.36.

In *In re Kim* (Cho Hung Bank v Kim) (Bankr 9th Cir 1994) 163 BR 157, aff'd (9th Cir 1995) 62 F3d 1511, the Ninth Circuit adopted the bankruptcy appellate panel holding that under 11 USC §523(a)(2) the creditor does not have to show it advanced new money in reliance on the debtor's fraud—the creditor need only show that it failed to exercise collection remedies in reliance on the debtor's misrepresentations at the time the debtor convinced the creditor to renew or extend the loan.

Two recent cases discuss the standards for denying a discharge based on fraudulent financial statements. *In re Kirsh* (9th Cir 1992) 973 F2d 1454 holds that reliance on financial statements must be justified. *In re Siriani* (9th Cir 1992) 967 F2d 302 holds that the creditor must show that the fraud proximately caused the loss and prove causation with evidence of reliance. But see *In re Yarbrow* (Bankr 9th Cir 1993) 150 BR 233 (FDIC as receiver for failed financial institution excused from requirement to show reliance on debtor's representations in dischargeability action under 11 USC §523(a)(2)(A); court applied *D'Oench, Duhme* doctrine).

In *In re Bugna* (9th Cir 1994) 33 F3d 1054, the Ninth Circuit held that a punitive damages award in a state court judgment was not dischargeable under §523(a)(4) when the punitive damages were based upon a breach of fiduciary duty.

The Ninth Circuit has also held that the punitive damage portion of a fraud claim held nondischargeable under 11 USC §523(a)(2) can be discharged. *In re Levy* (9th Cir 1991) 951 F2d 196. But see *In re Britton* (9th Cir 1991) 950 F2d 602; *In re Giangrasso* (Giangrasso v Butler) (Bankr 9th Cir 1992) 145 BR 319 (punitive damages were nondischargeable under 11 USC §523(a)(6) when based upon willful and malicious injury).

Failure to serve a nondischargeability complaint on both debtor and debtor's counsel may render the complaint time barred. *In re Bloomingdale* (Bankr CD Cal 1991) 137 BR 351. Conversely, failure to schedule a creditor and notify it of the case may result in the debt being excepted from discharge. *In re Haga* (Bankr WD Tex 1991) 131 BR 320.

REPRESENTING UNSECURED CREDITORS IN A BANKRUPTCY CASE

Offensive Tactics

[§10.36] Complaint To Determine Discharge and Dischargeability

If the 60-day period under Fed R Bankr P 4004(a) and 4007(c) to file a complaint objecting to discharge expires on a weekend or holiday, the bar date will be extended to the next day the court is open. *In re Burns* (Leisure Dev., Inc. v Burns) (Bankr 9th Cir 1989) 102 BR 750.

Generally, the 60-day period for filing a complaint to determine the dischargeability of a debt under 11 USC §523 runs from the first date set for the meeting of creditors, whether or not the meeting actually takes place. However, if the order setting the date is *vacated*, the filing deadline then begins to run from the date that the bankruptcy court subsequently sets for the creditor's meeting. *In re Burke* (Leisure Dev., Inc. v Burke) (Bankr 9th Cir 1989) 95 BR 716.

Burke must be reconciled with *In re Gordon* (9th Cir 1993) 988 F2d 1000, however, which held that when the meeting is *continued* to a later date, the deadline for filing the nondischargeability complaint is calculated from the date *first set* for the meeting, even though the meeting did not actually occur on that date. In view of *Gordon,* it is unclear if *Burke* is still good law. But see *In re Anwiler* (9th Cir 1992) 958 F2d 925 (court has equitable power to correct a notice that contains the wrong bar date for filing the complaint). See also *In re Kennerley* (9th Cir 1993) 995 F2d 145 (deadline for filing complaint was not satisfied by creditor's filing for or obtaining relief from automatic stay to sue debtor for fraud in state court) and *In re Begue* (Bankr ND Ohio 1995) 176 BR 801 (deadline for filing complaint was equitably tolled so that complaint mailed eight days before the deadline but received one day after it was considered timely.)

A creditor who is not listed on the debtor's schedules and who fails to receive formal notice of the deadline for filing a complaint to determine dischargeability is not entitled to file a late nondischargeability complaint if actual notice of the debtor's bankruptcy filing was received before the deadline. *In re Price* (9th Cir 1989) 871 F2d 97. *Price* means that an unscheduled creditor with actual notice of the bankruptcy filing has a duty to inquire regarding the bar date for filing a nondischargeability complaint. But *Price* involved a creditor who had received 58 days' notice. If the creditor had far less time, the rule of *Price* would be unfair. In *In re DeWalt* (Manufacturers Hanover v DeWalt) (9th Cir 1992) 961 F2d 848, the Ninth Circuit held that a creditor is ordinarily entitled to at least 30 days' advance notice of the bar date for filing a complaint to determine dischargeability. Because the creditor in *DeWalt* had only seven calendar days' notice, the complaint was not time barred.

Under Fed R Bankr P 4007(c) and 9006(b)(3), the bankruptcy court no longer has discretion to enlarge the time for filing complaints objecting to dischargeability if the request for an extension is made *after* the deadline for filing the complaint. See *In re De la Cruz* (Bankr 9th Cir 1994) 176 BR 19. However, the discussion in *In re Magouirk* (9th Cir 1982) 693 F2d 948, cited in Book §10.36, regarding the varying standards of "excusable neglect" still appears to be valid as it applies to requests to file late proofs of claim in Chapter 11 proceedings. *In re Dix* (Bankr 9th Cir 1988) 95 BR 134, 137 n2. For further discussion of *In re Dix,* see Update §10.41. The availability of the excusable neglect provision of Fed R Bankr P 9006(b)(1) for late-filed proofs of claim was confirmed by the Supreme Court in *Pioneer Inv. Servs. Co. v Brunswick Assocs. Ltd. Partnership* (1993) 507 US 380, 123 L Ed 2d 74, 113 S Ct 1489, discussed in Update §10.41.

Arguably, a natural disaster or other condition that makes it truly impossible to file a complaint or request an extension before the expiration of the bar date would give the court discretion to extend the deadline of Fed R Bankr P 4007(c) and 9006(b)(3). *In re Brown* (Merenda v Brown) (Bankr 9th Cir 1989) 102 BR 187, 189 n3. See also *In re Anwiler* (9th Cir 1992) 958 F2d 925, in which the Ninth Circuit held that the bankruptcy court could extend the deadline when the creditors were given the wrong bar date.

A creditor with a nondischargeability judgment does not have to obtain relief from the automatic stay to execute on the property acquired by the debtor postpetition that is not part of the bankruptcy estate. *In re Watson* (Bankr 9th Cir 1987) 78 BR 232. However, a creditor may not enforce a nondischargeability judgment against property in the estate without first obtaining relief from the stay. *In re Watson* (CD Cal 1987) 78 BR 267.

[§10.37] Involuntary Petitions

The 1994 Act amends 11 USC §303(b)(1) and (2) to increase the aggregate claim amount for petitioning creditors from $5000 to $10,000.

A debtor's sole remedy for an involuntary petition filed in bad faith is an action under 11 USC §303(i). Section 303(i) preempts state law permitting causes of action for abuse of process and malicious prosecution. *Gene R. Smith Corp. v Terry's Tractor, Inc.* (1989) 209 CA3d 951, 257 CR 598. See also *Idell v Goodman* (1990) 224 CA3d 262, 273 CR 605. See also *Landon v Hunt* (3d Cir 1992) 977 F2d 829, in which sanctions were awarded against petitioning creditors and their counsel on the grounds that the petition was filed in bad faith, because the debts were both contingent and subject to a bona fide dispute.

At least one circuit has challenged the single creditor rule adopted by many courts (there cannot be an involuntary bankruptcy case when the debtor has just one creditor). In *In re Concrete Plumbing Serv., Inc.* (6th Cir 1991) 943 F2d 627, the Sixth Circuit held that a single creditor can commence an involuntary bankruptcy in the event of debtor fraud. Recently, in *In re Kidwell* (Bankr ED Cal 1993) 158 BR 203, the bankruptcy court refused to dismiss an involuntary petition when the sole petitioning creditor misrepresented the number of the debtor's creditors to circumvent the three petitioning creditors requirement of 11 USC §303. Significantly, three other creditors opposed the dismissal and asked to join in the petition. The court indicated that sanctions could be obtained against the original petitioner if the case were eventually dismissed.

In *Atlas Mach. & Iron Works, Inc. v Bethlehem Steel Corp.* (4th Cir 1993) 986 F2d 709, the court refused to permit a petitioning creditor who filed the petition in bad faith to amend the petition to correct the defect. The petitioner admitted it had filed the case to collect its debt, which the court held was not a proper purpose for an involuntary petition.

[§10.38] Creditors' Committees

The 1994 Act made two changes that affect creditors' committees. First, new 11 USC §1102(a)(3) permits the court to dispense with a committee in a "small business" case. "Small business" is defined in new 11 USC §101(51C) as a business (other than one that primarily owns and operates real estate) whose debts do not exceed $2 million. Second, members of the committee may now be reimbursed for out-of-pocket expenses under new 11 USC §503(b)(3)(F).

A case with potentially far-reaching implications for creditors' committees is *Luedke v Delta Airlines, Inc.* (SD NY 1993) 159 BR 385. Former Pan Am employees had sued Delta for allegedly breaching a contract to fund Pan Am's reorganization. Delta filed a third party complaint against the committee of unsecured creditors of Pan Am seeking contribution. Essentially, Delta alleged that the creditors' committee interfered with the proposed contract between Pan Am and Delta and thereby brought about the demise of the contract. The committee moved to dismiss the third party complaint on the grounds that the committee was immune from suit for acts committed within the scope of its statutory duty. The district court denied the committee's motion and held that the immunity only covers actions taken within the scope of the committee's authority "as conferred by statute or the court" and does not extend to willful misconduct. 159 BR at 393.

[§10.39] Reclamation

The reference to Fed R Bankr P 7065(b) in the last paragraph of Book §10.39 is in error. The correct reference is to Fed R Bankr P 7054(b).

The 1994 Act amended §546(c)(1) to give the reclaiming seller more time to reclaim goods. The written demand to reclaim goods must now be made within 10 days of the debtor's receipt of the goods, but if the 10-day period expires after the date of the commencement of the case, the reclaiming seller now has 20 days after the debtor's receipt of the goods to make the written demand.

The 1994 Act also added §546(h), which will enable the trustee or debtor in possession to return the goods to the creditor, following notice and a hearing (and with the creditor's consent), and offset the price of the goods against the creditor's claim.

The definition of "insolvent" is now found in 11 USC §101(32).

An Article 9 security interest will defeat a seller's reclamation rights. *U.S. v Westside Bank* (5th Cir 1984) 732 F2d 1258; *In re Samuels* (Stowers v Mahon) (5th Cir 1984) 526 F2d 1238. It is also well settled that a proper reclamation claim is not avoidable by the bankruptcy trustee. *In re Daylin, Inc.* (9th Cir 1979) 596 F2d 853; *In re Telemart Enters.* (9th Cir 1975) 524 F2d 761. It is doubtful, however, that a reclaiming seller can reclaim proceeds of its goods. Even if the bankruptcy court denies reclamation, 11 USC §546(c)(2) permits an administrative priority claim to protect the reclaiming seller. *In re Coast Trading Co.* (9th Cir 1984) 744 F2d 686.

[§10.40] Postpetition Perfection of Certain Interests in Debtor's Property

A mechanics' lien can be recorded or a stop notice served after the bankruptcy case begins because, under California law, the perfected interest relates back to the time when work on the construction project began. 11 USC §362(b)(3); *In re KDR Bldg. Specialties, Inc.* (Bankr SD Cal 1987) 76 BR 778.

Although a mechanics' lien can be recorded or a stop notice served after a bankruptcy petition is filed by a contractor, an action to foreclose a mechanics' lien or to enforce a stop notice cannot be filed without relief from the automatic stay. The deadline for filing such an action is tolled by 11 USC §108(c). *In re Hunters Run Ltd. Partnership* (9th Cir 1989) 875 F2d 1425 (interpreting Washington law); see also *Rogers v Corrosion Prods., Inc.* (5th Cir 1995) 42 F3d 292.

The 1994 Act's amendment to 11 USC §546(b), which permits certain postpetition actions by secured creditors to maintain or accomplish perfection of security interests, is discussed in Update §10.28.

[§10.41] Proofs of Claim

The validity of a claim in a bankruptcy case is determined by the underlying state law. *In re Franklin* (Franklin v Commonwealth Fin. Corp.) (9th Cir 1991) 922 F2d 536.

The 1994 Act added 11 USC §502(b)(9) to provide that tardiness is now a ground for disallowance of a claim, except as provided under

11 USC §726(a)(1), (2), or (3), and except that governmental units will have 180 days from the date of the order for relief, or such later time as the Federal Rules of Bankruptcy Procedure provide, to file their claims. Fed R Bankr P 3002(c)(1) gives governmental units 180 days from the date of the order for relief to file claims.

For a discussion of late-filed priority tax claims in Chapter 7 cases, see discussion in Update §10.11.

Most of the circuit courts now hold that class proofs of claim are valid. *In re Charter Co.* (11th Cir 1989) 876 F2d 866; *Reid v White Motor Corp.* (6th Cir 1989) 886 F2d 1462; *In re American Reserve* (7th Cir 1988) 840 F2d 487. The Ninth Circuit has not ruled on this issue. See *In re Birting Fisheries, Inc.* (WD Wash 1995) 178 BR 849.

If a request for an extension of time to file a proof of claim is made *before* the deadline, the bankruptcy court may grant the request on a showing of "cause." If the request is made *after* the deadline, the request can be granted only on a showing of "excusable neglect." *In re Dix* (Bankr 9th Cir 1988) 95 BR 134. Citing *In re Magouirk* (9th Cir 1982) 693 F2d 948, the court in *Dix* stated that "excusable neglect" should be liberally construed to avoid foreclosing trial of a claim on its merits. The court identified five factors in determining whether there was excusable neglect (95 BR at 138): (1) whether granting the delay will prejudice the debtor; (2) the length of the delay and its impact on efficient court administration; (3) whether the delay was beyond the reasonable control of the person whose duty it was to perform; (4) whether the creditor acted in good faith; and (5) whether clients should be penalized for their counsel's neglect. The claim of excusable neglect must still be substantiated and weighed against the prejudice to the debtor and the other creditors occasioned by the delay.

The five factors outlined above were approved by the U.S. Supreme Court in *Pioneer Inv. Servs. Co. v Brunswick Assocs. Ltd. Partnership* (1993) 507 US 380, 123 L Ed 2d 74, 113 S Ct 1489, for the purpose of determining excusable neglect. The Court also held that "neglect" can include an inadvertent or even negligent omission. The creditors in *Pioneer* relied on their lawyer for filing their proof of claim, but the lawyer missed the bar date in the case, even though the notice was in both the lawyer's and the clients' files. Emphasizing the lack of prejudice to the debtor and the other creditors, the Court allowed the late claim. The decision was 5 to 4 and included a substantial dissent.

For a case distinguishing *Pioneer* and refusing to allow a late-filed claim, see *In re Bicoastal Corp.* (Bankr MD Fla 1994) 176 BR 966. For a case applying equitable standards for permitting a proof of claim to be filed late, see *In re Grivas* (Bankr SD Cal 1991) 123 BR 876.

The deadline under Fed R Bankr P 3002 for filing proofs of claim now applies to Chapter 12 family farmer debt adjustments, in addition to Chapter 7 and 13 proceedings. Fed R Bankr P 3002(c).

The informal proof of claim doctrine, discussed in Book §10.41, continues to be applied. See, *e.g.*, *In re Holm* (9th Cir 1991) 931 F2d 620.

The new proof of claim form replacing the one in Book §10.41 follows below.

B10 (Official Form 10)
(Rev. 1/95)

United States Bankruptcy Court
District of ____________

PROOF OF CLAIM

In re (Name of Debtor)

Case Number

NOTE: This form should not be used to make a claim for an administrative expense arising after the commencement of the case. A "request" for payment of an administrative expense may be filed pursuant to 11 U.S.C. § 503.

Name of Creditor
(The person or other entity to whom the debtor owes money or property)

Name and Address Where Notices Should be Sent

Telephone No.

[ ] Check box if you are aware that anyone else has filed a proof of claim relating to your claim. Attach copy of statement giving particulars.

[ ] Check box if you have never received any notices from the bankruptcy court in this case.

[ ] Check box if the address differs from the address on the envelope sent to you by the court.

THIS SPACE IS FOR COURT USE ONLY

ACCOUNT OR OTHER NUMBER BY WHICH CREDITOR IDENTIFIES DEBTOR:

Check here if this claim [ ] replaces [ ] amends a previously filed claim, dated:__________

1. BASIS FOR CLAIM
[ ] Goods sold
[ ] Services perfomed
[ ] Money loaned
[ ] Personal injury/wrongful death
[ ] Taxes
[ ] Other (Describe briefly)
[ ] Retiree benefits as defined in 11 U.S.C. § 1114(a)
[ ] Wages, salaries, and compensation (Fill out below)
Your social security number ____________
Unpaid compensation for services performed
from ____________ to ____________
(date) (date)

2. DATE DEBT WAS INCURRED

3. IF COURT JUDGMENT, DATE OBTAINED:

4. CLASSIFICATION OF CLAIM. Under the Bankruptcy Code all claims are classified as one or more of the following: (1) Unsecured nonpriority, (2) Unsecured Priority, (3) Secured. It is possible for part of a claim to be in one category and part in another.
CHECK THE APPROPRIATE BOX OR BOXES that best describe your claim and STATE THE AMOUNT OF THE CLAIM AT TIME CASE FILED.

[ ] SECURED CLAIM $
Attach evidence of perfection of security interest
Brief Description of Collateral:
[ ] Real Estate [ ] Motor Vehicle [ ] Other (Describe briefly)

Amount of arrearage and other charges at time case filed included in secured claim above, if any $

[ ] UNSECURED NONPRIORITY CLAIM $
A claim is unsecured if there is no collateral or lien on property of the debtor securing the claim or to the extent that the value of such property is less than the amount of the claim.

[ ] UNSECURED PRIORITY CLAIM $
Specify the priority of the claim.

[ ] Wages, salaries, or commissions (up to $4000),* earned not more than 90 days before filing of the bankruptcy petition or cessation of the debtor's business, whichever is earlier—11 U.S.C. § 507(a)(3)

[ ] Contributions to an employee benefit plan—11 U.S.C. § 507(a)(4)

[ ] Up to $1,800* of deposits toward purchase, lease, or rental of property or services for personal, family, or household use—11 U.S.C. § 507(a)(6)

[ ] Alimony, maintenance, or support owed to a spouse, former spouse, or child—11 U.S.C. § 507(a)(7)

[ ] Taxes or penalties of governmental units—11 U.S.C. § 507(a)(8)

[ ] Other—Specify applicable paragraph of 11 U.S.C. § 507(a)______
*Amounts are subject to adjustment on 4/1/98 and every 3 years thereafter with respect to cases commenced on or after the date of adjustment.

5. TOTAL AMOUNT OF CLAIM AT THE TIME CASE FILED $ ________ (Unsecured) $ ________ (Secured) $ ________ (Priority) $ ________ (Total)

[ ] Check this box if claim includes charges in addition to the principal amount of the claim. Attach itemized statement of all additional charges.

6. CREDITS AND SETOFFS: The amount of all payments on this claim has been credited and deducted for the purpose of making this proof of claim. In filing this claim, claimant has deducted all amounts that claimant owes to debtor.

7. SUPPORTING DOCUMENTS: Attach copies of supporting documents, such as promissory notes, purchase orders, invoices, itemized statements of running accounts, contracts, court judgments, or evidence of security interests. If the documents are not available, explain. If the documents are voluminous, attach a summary.

8. TIME STAMPED COPY: To receive an acknowledgement of the filing of your claim, enclose a stamped, self addressed envelope and copy of this proof of claim.

THIS SPACE IS FOR COURT USE ONLY

Date

Sign and print the name and title, if any, of the creditor or other person authorized to file this claim (attach copy of power of attorney, if any)

Penalty for presenting fraudulent claim: Fine of up to $500,000 or imprisonment for up to 5 years, or both. 18 U.S.C. §§ 152 and 3571.

[§10.43] Setoff

Although the automatic stay generally prevents a creditor from setting off mutual prepetition debts, the creditor can nevertheless institute an administrative freeze and refuse to pay its obligation to the debtor in order to maintain the status quo and preserve the creditor's rights under 11 USC §506(a) as a secured creditor entitled to adequate protection. See *In re Edgins* (Bankr 9th Cir 1984) 36 BR 480 (bank's administrative freeze of account does not violate stay). But see *In re Patterson* (11th Cir 1992) 967 F2d 505 (credit union's freeze of debtor's account violated automatic stay; creditor had other ways to protect its rights under Bankruptcy Code).

The equitable doctrine of recoupment might also be available to a creditor who wants to set off a prepetition claim against a postpetition claim, if the claims arise out of the same transaction. See, *e.g., In re Newbery Corp.* (Newbery Elec., Inc. v MCI Constr., Inc.) (Bankr 9th Cir 1992) 145 BR 998; *In re California Canners & Growers* (Bankr 9th Cir 1986) 62 BR 18. Recoupment is sometimes likened to a compulsory counterclaim, while setoff is compared to a permissive counterclaim.

A creditor with a claim entitled to setoff does not lose its setoff rights by failing to file a proof of claim before confirmation of the debtor's plan. See *In re De Laurentis Entertainment Group, Inc.* (9th Cir 1992) 963 F2d 1269. The court held that the creditor's right of setoff survived the debtor's discharge under 11 USC §1141 because 11 USC §553 takes precedence over §1141. But see *In re Cascade Roads, Inc.* (9th Cir 1994) 34 F3d 756, in which the United States was prevented by the bankruptcy court from asserting a setoff of the debtor's tax liability against its liability to the debtor. The court of appeals affirmed, holding that setoff is permissive, not mandatory, and the government's dilatory tactics in litigation warranted denial of setoff.

Defensive Tactics

Relief From Stay

[§10.45] Notice and Hearing

The changes made by the 1994 Act to 11 USC §362 are discussed at Update §10.27.

[§10.48] Executory Contracts and Unexpired Leases

The 1994 Act made three general changes to 11 USC §365. First, §365(b)(2)(D) provides that a breach of a nonmonetary obligation in an executory contract can be cured at a nondefault contract rate rather than the penalty rate. (For a case interpreting this language in the context of automobile franchise agreements, see *In re Claremont Acquisition Corp.* (Worthington v General Motors Corp.) (9th Cir 1997) 113 F3d 1029.)

Second, new §365(d)(10) now affords a lessor of personal property similar protections to those given lessors of real property. Under §365(d)(10), the trustee (debtor in possession) is required to timely perform obligations under the lease that arise 60 days after the entry of the order for relief. (Note that §365(d)(3), which applies to unexpired leases for nonresidential real property, covers the first 60 days of the case, while the payment requirement of §365(d)(10) only requires payment *after* the first 60 days of the case.) Third, §365(h) clarifies the rights of the lessee following rejection of an unexpired lease by the debtor-lessor.

As recently as 1992, the Ninth Circuit reiterated its adherence to the "Countryman test" for determining whether a contract is executory: A contract is executory when the obligations of both parties are so far unperformed that the failure of either party to complete performance would constitute a material breach and thus excuse the performance of the other. *In re Texscan Corp.* (9th Cir 1992) 976 F2d 1269, 1272. See also *In re Quintex Entertainment, Inc.* (9th Cir 1991) 950 F2d 1492.

For a different view, see *In re Drexel Burnham Lambert* (Bankr SD NY 1992) 138 BR 687, citing several law review articles in an attempt to develop a utilitarian approach to the issue.

Special rules apply to a lessee's duty to timely perform its postpetition obligations under an unexpired lease of nonresidential property. See 11 USC §365(d)(3). Generally, the obligations must be paid pending assumption or rejection of the lease. On a showing of cause, the trustee/debtor in possession can postpone performance for up to 60 days.

In *In re Pacific-Atlantic Trading Co.* (9th Cir 1994) 27 F3d 401, the Ninth Circuit held that a landlord is entitled to a claim with administrative priority for the full amount of the rent reserved under the lease from the date of filing through the date of rejection, regardless of whether the premises are being used by the debtor. The court declined to discuss whether the lessor's claim was entitled to superpriority status. Indeed, the requirement that the postpetition obligations be paid has created some confusion over whether a claim under 11 USC §365(d)(3) is entitled to "superpriority" over other postpetition payments, especially if the estate is administratively insolvent.

Under 11 USC §365(d)(4), an unexpired lease of nonresidential real property under which the debtor is the lessee is automatically terminated unless the debtor/trustee assumes or rejects the lease before expiration of 60 days from the date of the commencement of the case or assumes or rejects the lease within such other time period as the court may set for cause "within such 60 day period." This last phrase has led to confusion about whether the motion to extend the 60-day period had to be decided within the 60-day period or merely filed with the court before the end of the 60-day period. In the Ninth Circuit, it is settled that a motion filed within the 60-day period preserves the right to seek the extension, even if it is decided after expiration of the period. *In re Southwest Aircraft Servs., Inc.* (9th Cir 1987) 831 F2d 848; see also *In re Victoria Station, Inc.* (9th Cir 1989) 875 F2d 1380; *In re Victoria Station, Inc.* (9th Cir 1988) 840 F2d 682.

See also *In re Prize Frize, Inc.* (9th Cir 1994) 32 F3d 426 and *In re Argonaut Fin. Servs. Inc.* (ND Cal 1994) 164 BR 107. In *Prize Frize,* the court held that under §365(n)(1)(B), governing the rights of a licensee under a technology license following rejection by the debtor-licensor, the licensee must continue to make "royalty" payments as required in the license if the licensee elects to continue to use the license, regardless of whether the royalties are called royalties or license fees in the subject contract. *Argonaut* discusses the constitutional right to notice in instances where the deemed rejection provisions of §365(d)(4) operate to cut off valuable property rights.

[§10.49] Reorganization Plans

Classification of claims and other plan confirmation issues are discussed in greater detail in Update §10.17.

One notable change in the plan confirmation area made by the 1994 Act was the repeal of former 11 USC §1124(3). Former 11 USC §1124(3) provided that a creditor's claim was unimpaired if the creditor was paid the "allowed amount" of its claim. The "allowed amount" is defined in 11 USC §502 to be the amount of the prepetition claim without postpetition interest. Pursuant to 11 USC §1126(f), unimpaired creditors are deemed to have accepted the plan and, therefore, do not vote on the plan. Accordingly, the court never gets to the cramdown provisions of §1129(b) because the plan's confirmation is "consensual." Complicating matters, §1129(a)(7) enables any individual creditor to oppose confirmation if it will not receive at least as much as it would receive in a Chapter 7 liquidation conducted on the effective date of the plan and §728(a)(5) permits payment of interest if the estate is solvent. A further complication arises if the debtor is solvent on a reorganization value basis (*i.e.*, valued on future earnings), but insolvent on a "lights-out" liquidation basis. In *In re New Valley Corp.* (Bankr D NJ 1994) 168 BR 73, the court used the strict language of former §1124(3) to conclude that a solvent debtor's plan that paid general unsecured prepetition claims in cash without postpetition interest did not impair those creditors' claims. The 1994 Act changes this result by deleting former §1124(3). Now, creditors who are not paid postpetition interest by a solvent debtor are impaired and thus are entitled to vote. For a case interpreting this change to §1124, see *In re Atlanta-Stewart Partners* (Equitable Life Ins. Co. v Atlanta-Stewart Partners) (Bankr ND Ga 1996) 193 BR 79.

The 1994 Act also overruled *Rake v Wade* (1993) 508 US 464, 124 L Ed 2d 424, 113 S Ct 2187, by the addition of §1123(d). *Rake* held that interest must be paid by a debtor during a mortgage arrearage, thus effectively requiring the payment of interest on interest.

A plan that negatively amortizes the secured creditor's claim is not per se impermissible. *Great Western Bank v Sierra Woods Group* (9th Cir 1992) 953 F2d 1174. The court in *Great Western Bank* cited a list of factors to determine the fairness of a plan that includes negative amortization. These factors include the ratio of debt to value and adequate safeguards to the creditor. 953 F2d at 1178. See *In re Boulders on the River, Inc.* (Pacific First Bank v Boulders on the River, Inc.) (Bankr 9th Cir 1994) 164 BR 99 (debtor's plan to restructure construction loan was not filed in bad faith; confirmation of plan was affirmed); but see *In re Tri Growth Centre City, Ltd.* (Bankr SD Cal 1992) 136 BR 148, in which the court held that a plan's conversion of short-term debt to long-term debt was not fair and equitable because the lender never bargained for a long-term loan or the shifting of the risk of declining hotel business onto the lender.

[§10.50] Trustee's and Debtor's Avoiding Powers

Until the 1994 Act, there was considerable confusion over the proper time period within which to bring an avoiding action under 11 USC §§544, 545, 547, 548, or 553. Although the language of §546(a) seemed clear, the case law was confusing. Under former 11 USC §546(a), an action had to be commenced before the earlier of two years after the appointment of a trustee under 11 USC §§702, 1104, 1163, 1202, or 1302, or the time the case was closed or dismissed. Based on the plain language of former §546(a), most practitioners thought that when no trustee had been appointed, the time for bringing a preference action did not expire after two years as long as the case had not been closed or dismissed. In spite of this, the court came to a contrary conclusion in *In re Softwaire Centre Int'l, Inc.* (9th Cir 1993) 994 F2d 682, which held that the debtor in possession was barred from bringing a preference action because the action had not been brought within two years of the commencement of the case. See also *In re San Joaquin Roast Beef* (9th Cir 1993) 7 F3d 1413 (Chapter 7 trustee's actions were time-barred under §546(a), not because of the expiration of two years from the commencement of the Chapter 11 case as suggested by the *Softwaire Centre* rationale, but because two years had elapsed from the appointment of the previous Chapter 11 trustee). See also *In re IRFM, Inc.* (Mosier v Kroger) (9th Cir 1995) 65 F3d 778; *In re Hanna* (John Mitchell, Inc. v Steinbrugge) (9th Cir 1995) 72 F3d 114.

Under revised §546(a), actions under §§544, 545, 547, 548, or 553 may be brought until the later of (i) two years after the entry of the order for relief, (ii) one year after election or appointment of the first trustee in the case, if such election or appointment occurs within two years of entry of the order for relief, or (iii) the time the case is closed or dismissed. The legislative history indicates that tolling agreements are permitted and that equitable tolling based on fraud is still available to extend the time periods.

Title 11 USC §550 permits preferences and fraudulent transfers to be recovered from a party for whose benefit the transfer was made as well as from the party who received the transfer. Under certain circumstances, later transferees can also be held liable. 11 USC §550(b)(1). In *In re Bullion Reserve* (9th Cir 1991) 922 F2d 544, the Ninth Circuit held that absent a showing of specific intent to make the transfer for the benefit of such person, a later transferee cannot be a person for whose benefit the initial transfer was made and that a party who never had control over the transferred funds cannot be a "transferee" under the statute.

Under 11 USC §502(d), the court must disallow a claim of an entity that is a transferee of a transfer avoidable under any of the trustee's avoiding powers. However, §502(d) does not require a transfer to be avoided in order to bar the creditor's other claims. *In re KF Dairies, Inc.* (Bankr 9th Cir 1992) 143 BR 734 (time-barred action for avoidance of postpetition transfer could still furnish grounds for objection to creditor's claim).

The references to §§10.23–10.27 in Book §10.50 should be to §§10.51–10.55.

[§10.51] Preferences

Trust fund taxes (*e.g.*, withholding or sales taxes) voluntarily paid before the filing of a bankruptcy case cannot be recovered as a preference. *Begier v IRS* (1990) 496 US 53, 110 L Ed 2d 46, 110 S Ct 2258. The Court concluded that such voluntary transfers were not "property of the debtor," even though they had not been held in a segregated tax account, because the funds in question became trust funds when they were paid.

Payments on long-term debt, as well as on short-term debt, can qualify for the "ordinary course of business" exception to the trustee's power to avoid preferential transfers. *Union Bank v Wolas* (1991) 502 US 151, 116 L Ed 2d 514, 112 S Ct 527.

A frequently litigated issue in preference actions is when a transfer by check is considered to occur. In *Barnhill v Johnson* (1992) 503 US 393, 118 L Ed 2d 39, 112 S Ct 1386, the Supreme Court held that for the purpose of 11 USC §547 a transfer by check occurs on the date it is *honored* by the bank, rather than on the date it is delivered to the payee. However, the Ninth Circuit has held that the date of transfer of a cashier's check is the date of delivery. *In re Lee* (Hall-Mark Elecs. Corp. v Sims) (9th Cir 1997) 108 F3d 239. In *In re Kemp Pac. Fisheries, Inc.* (9th Cir 1994) 16 F3d 313, the Ninth Circuit addressed whether the debtor's property is transferred for purposes of §547(b)(1) when the bank honors a check to a creditor even though the debtor has insufficient funds in its account to cover the check. The court treated the overdraft as a loan and held that the proceeds of the loan were property of the debtor. *In re Grand Chevrolet* (9th Cir 1994) 25 F3d 728 discusses the concept of a contemporaneous exchange for value, which is an exception found in §547(c)(1).

The 1994 Act overruled the *Deprizio* decision (*Levit v Ingersoll Rand Fin. Corp.* (7th Cir 1989) 874 F2d 1186). New §550(c) provides that if a transfer that occurred between 90 days and one year of the petition date that benefited an insider is avoided under §547(b), the trustee may not recover the transfer from a creditor that is *not* an insider. For cases that examine when an individual will be deemed an insider under 11 USC §547(b)(4)(B), see *In re Friedman* (Bankr 9th Cir 1991) 126 BR 63, and *In re Standard Stores, Inc.* (Bankr CD Cal 1991) 124 BR 318.

To come within the ordinary course of business defense to a preference action under 11 USC §547(c)(2)(C), the conduct must be judged according to an objective standard. It is not enough that the transfer might have been consistent with the debtor's and creditor's past dealings. The statute requires proof that the challenged transfer would be deemed ordinary by businesses similarly situated to the debtor and the transferee. *In re Loretto Winery, Ltd.* (Bankr 9th Cir 1989) 107 BR 707.

[§10.52] Fraudulent Transfers

A regularly conducted foreclosure sale is not a fraudulent transfer and irrebuttably establishes that a fair price was received for the property. *BFP v Resolution Trust Corp.* (1994) 511 US ___, 128 L Ed 2d 556, 114 S Ct 1757.

For Ninth Circuit rulings on fraudulent conveyances as applied to leveraged buy-outs, see *Lippi v City Bank* (9th Cir 1992) 955 F2d 599; *Kupetz v Wolf & Vine* (9th Cir 1988) 845 F2d 842.

[§10.55] Liens That Impair Exemptions

The 1994 Act amended 11 USC §522(f)(2) to provide a mathematical definition of impairment for purposes of determining whether a judicial lien impairs an exemption. A lien impairs an exemption to the extent that the sum of (1) the lien, plus (2) all other liens on the property, plus (3) the amount of the debtor's exemption if there were no liens, exceeds the value of the debtor's interest in the absence of any liens. This new statutory formula overrules cases such as *In re Chabot* (9th Cir 1993) 992 F2d 891, by removing a partially secured judicial lien to the extent necessary to preserve the entire amount of the exemption. *Chabot* continues to apply to cases filed before October 22, 1994. See *In re Wilson* (Wynns v Wilson) (9th Cir 1996) 90 F3d 347.

The 1994 Act also provides greater protection to alimony, maintenance, and support obligations of a debtor to his or her spouse, former spouse, or children by providing under §522(f)(1)(A) that under particular circumstances, liens that protect such payments are not subject to avoidance under §522(f). Similarly, under §522(f)(3), if the debtor uses the state-law exemptions, nonpossessory nonpurchase-money liens on items such as implements, professional tools, and tools of trade are not avoidable to the extent the value of such items exceeds $5000.

Title 11 USC §522(f)(1) does not permit a debtor to avoid a lien on a homestead when the lien is granted to a former spouse under a divorce decree and the lien secures the nondebtor spouse's former interest. *Farrey v Sanderfoot* (1991) 500 US 291, 114 L Ed 2d 337, 111 S Ct 1825. The Court ruled that 11 USC §522(f)(1) only permits the avoidance of a lien when the lien attaches to the debtor's interest *after* the debtor obtained the interest. The debtor in *Farrey* never had an interest in his former wife's undivided half interest in their home, *i.e.,* the property subject to the lien, *until* the debtor's marriage was dissolved and the former spouse obtained a lien on her share of the property. Thus, he could not avoid a lien fixed on that half interest of the property.

Relying on *Farrey v Sanderfoot, supra,* the Bankruptcy Appellate Panel for the Ninth Circuit has held that a Chapter 7 debtor's former spouse's lien on the marital residence was not avoidable because the lien was created as part of the divorce decree, which created "new" property interests. The debtor did not have an interest in the property until after the lien attached to it. *In re Yerrington* (Bankr 9th Cir 1992) 144 BR 96. A similar result was reached in *In re Catli* (9th Cir 1993) 999 F2d 1405 (Chapter 7 debtor unsuccessfully tried to avoid lien on marital residence for one-half sale proceeds granted to his wife in divorce proceedings). See also *In re Parrish* (5th Cir 1993) 7 F3d 76.

Before 11 USC §522(f) may be utilized to avoid a lien, there must be an exemption to which the debtor would have been entitled. An exemption that is "valid" only because the creditor failed to object does not satisfy this requirement. *In re Morgan* (Bankr 9th Cir 1993) 149 BR 147. The debtor in *Morgan* claimed a homestead exemption against property subject to a judicial lien. The creditor failed to file a timely objection to the exemption. Relying on *Taylor v Freeland & Kronz* (1992) 503 US 638, 118 L Ed 2d 280, 112 S Ct 1644, discussed in Update §10.20, the debtor argued that, because the objection was time barred and the lien impaired the claimed exemption, the lien could be avoided. The court rejected this argument, reasoning that an exemption obtained by default under §522(*l*) does not necessarily entitle the debtor to the exemption under §522(b).

11

Third Party Claims

INTRODUCTION

[§11.3] Chart: Procedural Guide to Third Party Claims

The time in which the petitioner must serve notice of the hearing on the validity of the third party claim is now governed by CCP §1005(b). CCP §720.320(a). For discussion of requirements under CCP §1005(b), see Update §4.24.

PROCEDURE

Hearing on Claim

Notice of Hearing

[§11.32] Service; Content

See Update §11.3.

[§11.36] Pleadings; Hearing; Appeal

In *Whitehouse v Six Corp.* (1995) 40 CA4th 527, 48 CR2d 600, the court held that when a creditor in a third party claim procedure resists the claim by asserting the property has been fraudulently transferred to the third party, the creditor must prove this allegation by a preponderance of the evidence. The court also discussed the limitations on discovery and the right to a jury trial in a third party claim procedure. See also *Regency Outdoor Advertising, Inc. v Carolina Lanes, Inc.* (1995) 31 CA4th 1323, 37 CR2d 552.

12

Lien Priorities; Preferred Labor Claims

LIEN PRIORITIES

Judgment Lien on Real Property

[§12.2] Creation and Duration; Modification

On the necessity of reducing a sister-state judgment to a California judgment by complying with the Sister State Money Judgments Act (CCP §§1710.10–1710.65), see *Kahn v Berman* (1988) 198 CA3d 1499, 244 CR 575, discussed in Update §6.45.

Former CCP §117 has been repealed. For small claims matters, see CCP §§116.110–116.950. For further discussion, see §2.24.

Money judgments for the payment of child, spousal, or family support or for reimbursement under Welf & I C §11350 do not need to be renewed. CCP §683.130(c)(1). The judgment creditor has the option, however, of renewing such judgments if the judgment has not been renewed regarding past due amounts or if five years has elapsed since the last renewal. CCP §683.130(c)(2).

A judgment lien created under CCP §697.320(a) based on a money judgment for child, family, or spousal support payable in installments continues during the period the judgment remains enforceable unless the money judgment is satisfied or the judgment lien is released. CCP §697.320(b).

Effective January 1, 1994, the former Family Law Act (former CC §§4000–5317) was repealed and replaced by the Family Code.

[§12.3] Property Subject to Lien

Under CCP §697.340(a), a judgment lien will not affect previously transferred property. Accordingly, an executed and delivered but unrecorded quitclaim deed conveys title free and clear of a later recorded abstract of judgment. *Casey v Gray* (1993) 13 CA4th 611, 16 CR2d 538.

[§12.7] Release or Subordination of Judgment Lien

Operative January 1, 1988, an amendment to CCP §697.370(b) requires that the release, instead of describing the property being released, must contain a statement substantially as follows:

> This is a release from the judgment lien described herein of all the interests in real property in ______________ County presently owned or hereafter acquired of the herein named judgment debtor subject to the lien.

This requirement applies if all the judgment debtor's real property, in a county where the lien is recorded, is being released from the judgment lien or if the judgment debtor does not have any known interest in any real property in that county. CCP §697.370(b).

Judgment Lien on Business Personal Property

[§12.9] Creation and Duration

Former CCP §117 has been repealed and replaced by CCP §116.620, providing for the satisfaction of small claims judgments by installment payments.

[§12.14] Priority Between Judgment Lien on Personal Property and Security Interest

The 10-day grace period under CCP §697.590(d) has been increased to 20 days.

[§12.17] Release, Subordination, or Acknowledgment of Satisfaction of Judgment Lien on Personal Property

Code of Civil Procedure §697.650(a) has been amended to permit the judgment creditor, by a writing, to release the judgment lien on all the personal property subject to the lien of a sole judgment debtor or of all the judgment debtors. CCP §697.650(a)(1). When a notice of judgment lien names more than one judgment debtor, the judgment creditor may release, by a writing, the judgment lien on all the personal property of one or more, but fewer than all, the judgment debtors. CCP §697.650(a)(2). Matters found in former CCP §697.650(a)(1)–(2) are now found in CCP §697.650(a)(3)–(4) respectively. The statement of release or subordination must contain wording appropriate to bring the statement within one of the above paragraphs of CCP §697.650(a). CCP §697.650(b).

The provision governing the fee for filing the statement of release or subordination is now found in CCP §697.650(d). The filing fee under Com C §§9404 and 9405 has been increased to $20 if the statement is in the form prescribed by the Secretary of State. Otherwise, the fee is $30.

Execution Lien

[§12.19] Creation and Duration

To execute against property, a judgment creditor need not create a judgment lien first. "The creditor can simply choose to levy execution, thereby creating an execution lien." *Kahn v Berman* (1988) 198 CA3d 1499, 1507 n7, 244 CR 575.

[§12.20] Priority When Property Subject to Execution Lien Is Transferred or Encumbered

Code of Civil Procedure §697.740 provides that, with certain exceptions, personal property subject to an execution lien that is not in the levying officer's custody remains subject to the lien after it has been transferred, unless the transfer is made to one of the transferees listed in CCP §697.740(a)–(k). Code of Civil Procedure §697.740(c) includes a lessee in the ordinary course of business (as defined) as a protected transferee.

Code of Civil Procedure §697.740(f) now provides that a "protected purchaser," as defined in Com C §8303, rather than a "bona fide purchaser," is protected. "Protected purchaser" is defined in Com C §8303 as a purchaser who gives value, without notice of any adverse claim, and obtains control of the security. A protected purchaser acquires its interest free of any adverse claim. Com C §8303.

Code of Civil Procedure §697.740(a) provides that a person who acquires an interest in property under California law for reasonably equivalent value without knowledge of the lien takes the property free of the lien. For purposes of this subdivision, value is given if, in exchange for the transfer or encumbrance, property is transferred or an antecedent debt is secured or satisfied.

On the enforcement of a money judgment against property subject to a lien after it is transferred or encumbered, see CCP §695.070, discussed in Update §7.13.

[§12.21] Enforcement of Security Interest When Property Levied on Not in Levying Officer's Custody

Code of Civil Procedure §701.040(b) has been amended to provide that, after the security interest is satisfied, the secured party must deliver any excess property and pay any excess payments or proceeds to the levying officer for the purpose of the levy as provided in Com C §§9502 and 9504 unless the court or the levying officer directs otherwise.

[§12.22] Other Enforcement Liens; Priority

The cross-reference to §§9.5–9.33 in Book §12.22 should be to §§8.5–8.33. Similarly, the cross-references to §§9.35–9.40 and to §§9.41–9.44 should be to §§8.35–8.40 and §§8.41–8.44, respectively.

[§12.23] Priority Between Lien Creditor and Perfected or Unperfected Security Interest

The time period within which the secured party must file a financing statement for a purchase money security interest to take priority has been increased from 10 to 20 days after the debtor receives possession of the collateral. Com C §9301(2).

[§12.25] Priority When Competing State Tax Lien Involved

Former Fish & G C §8048 was repealed in 1986.

Former Rev & T C §26161 was repealed in 1993 and replaced by Rev & T C §19221, operative January 1, 1994.

Effective January 1, 1995, Rev & T C §6757 was added to clarify that the lien provided by that section does not arise during any period that the automatic stay of 11 USC §362 applies to the person against whom the lien would otherwise arise.

[§12.26] Priority Concerning Other Liens

When a lien on the proceeds of a lawsuit is created by contract, the validity of the lien is governed by CC §2881(1), even though the purpose of the lien is to secure payment of legal fees and the legal services for which the lien secures payment are not rendered in conjunction with the lawsuit. In addition, a creditor need not file notice of lien in the pending lawsuit to create the lien or to ensure priority over subsequent liens. *Bluxome Street Assocs. v Woods* (1988) 206 CA3d 1149, 254 CR 198. The rule of *Woods* applies to any contractual lien on the proceeds of an action, not only to liens to secure payment of legal services.

Table of Statutes, Regulations, and Rules: Book

The following statutes cited in the Book were omitted from the Book Table of Statutes. All statutes appear in Book chart §4.5.

CCP §482.100(c)
CCP §484.010
CCP §§484.010–484.110
CCP §484.040
CCP §484.060
CCP §484.070(a)
CCP §484.070(b)
CCP §484.070(e)
CCP §484.070(f)
CCP §484.090
CCP §484.090(b)
CCP §484.110
CCP §§484.310–484.370
CCP §§484.320–484.350
CCP §484.330
CCP §484.350
CCP §484.350(d)
CCP §484.360
CCP §484.360(a)
CCP §484.370
CCP §§485.010–485.240
CCP §485.210
CCP §485.510
CCP §§485.510–485.540
CCP §485.610(a)
CCP §485.610(b)
CCP §§486.010–486.110
CCP §486.010(a)
CCP §486.020
CCP §486.030
CCP §486.100
CCP §487.030(a)
CCP §489.230
CCP §489.310
CCP §489.310(a)
CCP §489.320
CCP §489.320(a)
CCP §489.410
CCP §489.410(a)
CCP §489.420
CCP §492.010
CCP §§492.010–492.020
CCP §492.020(a)
CCP §492.030
CCP §492.050
CCP §492.050(a)
CCP §492.050(c)
CCP §492.050(d)
CCP §492.060
CCP §492.090
CCP §703.520(a)
CCP §§921–922

Table of Statutes, Regulations, and Rules: Update

INTERNAL REVENUE CODE

ACTS BY POPULAR NAME

Table of Cases

C

X

Y

Z

Table of References

The following titles are additions to or replacements for the Book Table of References.

1–3 California Civil Procedure Before Trial (3d ed Cal CEB 1990) (replacing 2d edition cited in Book): §§1.1, 1.11, 1.18–1.19, 1.56, 2.1, 2.30, 3.1–3.2, 3.5, 3.7, 3.11, 3.25, 3.36–3.38, 3.41, 3.43–3.44, 3.49–3.51, 3.60, 3.67, 3.64, 3.69, 4.6, 5.41, 6.1, 6.9, 6.14, 6.19–6.21, 6.23–6.28, 6.35, 6.43,

California Civil Appellate Practice (3d ed Cal CEB 1996): §6.43

California Decedent Estate Practice Vols 1–2 (Cal CEB 1986); Vol 3 (Cal CEB 1987): §8.75

California Attorney Fee Awards (2d ed Cal CEB 1994): §2.20

2A California Forms of Pleading and Practice. Oakland: Matthew Bender & Co., 1992 (replacing 1986 edition cited in Book): §4.6

California Lis Pendens Practice (2d ed Cal CEB 1994): §5.38

California Marital Termination Agreements (Cal CEB 1988): §2.27

California Mechanics' Liens and Other Remedies (2d ed Cal CEB 1988) (replacing 1st edition cited in Book): §5.39

California Real Property Sales Transactions (2d ed Cal CEB 1993) (replacing 1st edition cited in Book): §§2.73, 2.108

California State Sheriffs' Association Civil Procedure Manual (4th ed rev 1994): §§3.38, 4.6, 4.43, 7.23

1–3 California Trial Practice: Civil Procedure During Trial (3d ed Cal CEB 1995) (replacing California Civil Procedure During Trial, cited in Book): §§1.1, 2.1, 6.1–6.3, 6.29, 6.41, 6.44, 8.31

1, 2 Civil Discovery Practice in California (2d ed Cal CEB 1988) (replacing California Civil Discovery Practice (Cal CEB 1975)): §§4.6, 6.2–6.3, 8.34–8.34A

Collection Agency Laws, Rules, and Regulations. Sacramento, Calif.: Bureau of Collection and Investigative Services, 1982 (replacing Debt Collection Manual, cited in Book): §2.119

Corbin, A. L. Corbin on Contracts. St. Paul Minn., West Publishing Co. (rev ed 1993) (replacing edition cited in Book): §2.37

Litigation in the Fast Lane: Rules, Analysis, and Practice Guide for Local Programs Mandated Under the Trial Court Delay Reduction Act (Cal CEB 1988): §1.1

Los Angeles Law Department Policy Manual (former): §§4.26, 4.83, 6.15

Practice Under the California Family Code (Cal CEB annual): §1.1

Secured Transactions in California Commercial Law Practice (Cal CEB 1986): §4.53

Sommer, McGarity & King. Collier Family Law and the Bankruptcy Code. New York: Matthew Bender, 1991 (updated periodically)

Williston, Contracts (4th ed 1990): §2.37

Witkin, B. E. Summary of California Law. 13 vols. 9th ed. (supplemented). San Francisco: Bancroft-Whitney Co., 1987 (replacing 8th edition cited in Book): §2.37

Table of Forms: Update

Index: Update

The symbol "f" after a section number indicates that a form appears in the section.

Table of Forms: Book

This is the corrected version of the Book Table of Forms. References are to Book chapter section numbers.

Index: Book

This is the corrected version of the Book Index.
References are to Book chapter section numbers.

Make sure you are using the latest update

For your convenience, the following list identifies the most recent publication date of each CEB update (as of November 1997).

Update Title	Product Number	Publication Date
Advising California Condominium and Homeowners Associations	RE-31635	3/97
Advising California Employers, 2d Edition	BU-32031	5/97
Advising California Nonprofit Corporations	BU-36629	6/97
Advising California Partnerships, 2d Edition	BU-35639	5/97
Appeals and Writs in Criminal Cases	CR-33489	3/97
Attorney's Guide to California Construction Contracts and Disputes, 2d Edition	RE-31446	11/97
Attorney's Guide to California Professional Corporations, 4th Edition	TX-30939	5/97
Attorney's Guide to Pension and Profit-Sharing Plans, 3d Edition	TX-30737	9/97
Business Buy-Sell Agreements	BU-31495	3/97
California Administrative Mandamus, 2d Edition	CP-38817	4/97
California Attorney's Damages Guide	CP-31434	4/97
California Attorney Fee Awards, 2d Edition	CP-32163	9/97
California Automobile Insurance Law Guide	TO-30758	1/97
California Breach of Contract Remedies	CP-34467	9/97
California Business Practice Forms Manual	BU-31985	9/97
California Civil Appellate Practice, 3d Edition	CP-32431	5/97
California Civil Litigation Forms Manual	CP-34478	7/97
California Civil Procedure Before Trial, 3d Edition	CP-31546	5/97
California Civil Writ Practice, 3d Edition	CP-32781	5/97

Update Title	Product Number	Publication Date
California Commercial Law II	BU-30044	6/92
California Condominium and Planned Development Practice	RE-38873	4/97
California Conservatorships and Guardianships	ES-31504	5/97
California Criminal Law Forms Manual	CR-32151	9/97
California Criminal Procedure and Practice, 3d Edition	CR-32111	6/96
California Decedent Estate Practice 1, 2	ES-35669	5/97
California Decedent Estate Practice 3	ES-30869	5/97
California Durable Powers of Attorney	ES-32661	3/97
California Elder Law—An Advocate's Guide	ES-32054	6/97
California Eviction Defense Manual, 2d Edition	RE-32084	5/97
California Evidence Benchbook, 2d Edition	CP-32371	6/90
California Expert Witness Guide, 2d Edition	CP-31686	3/97
California Government Tort Liability Practice, 2d Edition	TO–31695	2/97
California Judges Benchbook: Criminal Trials	CR-31797	5/97
California Juvenile Court Practice, Volume 1	CR-35524	1/97
California Juvenile Court Practice, Volume 2	CR-35533	3/97
California Liability Insurance Practice 1, 2	CP-39266	8/97
California Local Probate Rules, 18th Edition	ES-39668	1/97
California Mechanics' Liens and Other Remedies, 2d Edition	RE-30998	11/96
California Mortgage and Deed of Trust Practice, 2d Edition	RE-31347	2/97
California Personal Injury Proof	TO-30561	6/97
California Probate Code Annotated to CEB Publications	ES-31198	1/97
California Probate Workflow Manual	ES-31567	6/97
California Real Property Financing, Volume 1	RE-30977	3/97
California Real Property Financing, Volume 2	RE-30897	5/97
California Real Property Practice Forms Manual	RE-30928	2/96

Update Title	Product Number	Publication Date
California Real Property Remedies Practice	RE-38867	11/97
California Real Property Sales Transactions, 2d Edition	RE-32094	9/96
California Subdivision Map Act Practice	RE-32351	4/97
California Tort Damages	TO-30888	1/97
California Tort Guide, 3d Edition	TO-32541	4/97
California Trial Objections, 5th Edition	CP-32552	5/97
California Trial Practice: Civil Procedure During Trial, 3d Edition	CP-32192	3/97
California Trust Administration	ES-31706	4/97
California Uninsured Motorist Practice	TO-30581	12/96
California Will Drafting, 3d Edition	ES–30325	5/97
California Workers' Compensation Practice, 3d Edition	WC-35621	5/97
California Workers' Damages Practice	WC-30772	5/97
California Zoning Practice	RE-30518	3/97
Civil Discovery Practice in California	CP-30767	11/97
Civil Trials Benchbook	CP-34558	12/95
Competitive Business Practices, 2d Edition	BU-31656	11/97
Condemnation Practice in California	RE-32412	6/97
Counseling California Corporations	BU-39236	5/97
Debt Collection Practice in California	BU-30811	12/97
Debt Collection Tort Practice	TO-30105	8/97
Drafting Agreements for the Sale of California Businesses, 3d Edition	BU-32791	5/97
Drafting Business Contracts: Principles, Techniques and Forms	BU-30801	12/96
Drafting California Revocable Living Trusts, 3d Edition	ES-32182	11/96
Effective Direct & Cross Examination	CP-32333	11/97
Effective Introduction of Evidence	CP-31356	5/97
Estate Planning Practice 1, 2	ES-30858	9/97
Fee Agreement Forms Manual	MI-30444	6/96
Financing California Businesses, 2d Edition	BU-32422	6/97
Forming & Operating California Limited Liability Companies	BU-32512	5/97
Ground Lease Practice	RE-30523	1/97
Guide to California Subdivision Sales Law	RE-31321	8/97
Landslide and Subsidence Liability	RE-31035	9/97
Lis Pendens, 2d Edition	RE-32173	8/97
Managing an Estate Planning Practice	ES-31942	7/96

Update Title	Product Number	Publication Date
Office Leasing: Drafting and Negotiating the Lease	RE-30891	2/97
Organizing Corporations in California, 2d Edition	BU-37763	5/97
Persuasive Opening Statements and Closing Arguments	CP-39658	11/97
Practice Under the California Environmental Quality Act	RE–30263	11/97
Practice Under the California Family Code: Dissolution, Legal Separation, Nullity	FA-31956	2/97
Practicing California Judicial Arbitration	CP-30664	11/97
Proof in Competitive Business Litigation	CP-31931	6/97
Real Property Exchanges, 2d Edition	RE-32133	6/97
Sales & Leases in California Commercial Law Practice	BU-32073	7/97
Secured Transactions in California Commercial Law Practice	BU-32319	3/97
Selecting & Forming Business Entities	BU-32571	6/97
Tax Aspects of California Partnerships	TX-37742	3/97
Tax Aspects of Marital Dissolutions, 2d Edition	TX-31336	6/96
Taxation of Real Property Transfers	RE-37752	12/96
Trial Attorney's Evidence Code Notebook, 3d Edition	CP-30294	3/97

Not Yet Updated	Product Number
California Administrative Hearing Practice, 2d Edition	CP-3267*
California Landlord-Tenant Practice, 2d Edition	RE-3269*
California Marital Settlement and Other Family Law Agreements	FA-3296*
California Title Insurance Practice, 2d Edition	RE-3262*
Capitalizing & Protecting New Businesses	BU-3294*
Drafting California Irrevocable Living Trusts, 3d Edition	ES-3271*
Jefferson's Synopsis of California Evidence Law	CP-3079*

Not Yet Updated	Product Number
Trade Secrets Practice in California, 2d Edition	BU-3259*
Wrongful Employment Termination Practice, 2d Edition	CP-3265*